9E

CW01090630

STUDIES IN THE U

The entrepreneur

Keith Glaister
Senior lecturer in Business Studies
at Huddersfield Polytechnic

HEINEMANN
EDUCATIONAL

Heinemann Educational,
a division of Heinemann Educational Books Ltd,
Halley Court, Jordan Hill, Oxford OX2 8EJ

OXFORD   LONDON   EDINBURGH
MELBOURNE   SYDNEY   AUCKLAND
SINGAPORE   MADRID   IBADAN
NAIROBI   GABORONE   HARARE
KINGSTON   PORTSMOUTH   NH   (USA)

First published 1989

British Library Cataloguing in Publication Data
Glaister, K. (Keith)
   The entrepreneur, – (Studies in the UK economy),
   1. Great Britain. Entrepreneurship
   I. Title II. Series
   338'.04'0041

ISBN   0 435 33007 1

Typeset and illustrated by Gecko Limited, Bicester, Oxon

Printed and bound in Great Britain by Biddles Ltd, King's Lynn and Guildford

Acknowledgements

I would like to thank Bryan Hurl for his help and encouragement during the preparation of this book.

Thanks are also due to the following for permission to reproduce copyright material: *Achiever News* for the material on pp. 2–3; Nick Baker for the cartoons on pp. 24 and 69; Ian Bradley for the article from *The Times* on pp.11–12; British Business for the profile on pp. 33–5 and the table on p. 62; The Controller of Her Majesty's Stationery Office for the table on p. 60; *Financial Times* for the articles on pp. 9–10, 72–3, 74–5; *Financial Weekly* for the pie diagram on p. 81 and the table on p. 82; *Guardian* for the article on pp. 55–6; *Investors Chronicle* for the profile on pp. 46–8; *Management Today* for the profile on pp. 56–8; Midland Bank for the tables on pp. 61 and 63; Small Firms Service for the excerpts on pp. 76–7; Times Newspapers Limited 1986 for the article on pp. 4–5.

Preface

I imagine that there are few secondary schools in the country now where the entrepreneur does not stalk the classrooms, either in the guise of pupils holding board meetings of their Young Enterprise firms; teams playing competitive computer business games; or thriving Careers Conventions where businessmen are welcomed. Evidently the assumed ageless Monopoly board game has been revamped to incorporate the entrepreneur, and has been renamed Polyopoly.

In Victorian times the entrepreneur was lauded generally as the enterpriser who had produced the industrial revolution and made Britain great. Yet for all this century – until the Thatcher years – his image has been cast down by the educational establishment. Even in economics texts for A and AS level the coverage is meagre. Now that the 'Thatcher Revolution' is with us it seems essential to rectify this with Keith Glaister's study for the *Studies in the UK Economy* series.

Bryan Hurl
Series Editor

Contents

Chapter One

Introduction

The entrepreneur plays an extremely important role in the operation of a market economy and yet has suffered relative neglect in the writing and teaching of introductory economics.

During the 1980s there has been a renewed interest in the entrepreneur and **entrepreneurship**. Since the Conservative party returned to power in 1979 it has made a clear display of promoting an 'enterprise culture' in Britain. The government has, for example, reduced direct taxation in order to encourage initiative and enterprise and to enhance the rewards of risk-taking. The government has provided tax relief for individuals who supply venture capital for new businesses under the Business Expansion Scheme. Allowances have also been provided for the unemployed to encourage them to start their own businesses. Associated with these government initiatives a great deal of advice and training has been made available for those who wish to start a business, provided for instance by the Department of Trade and Industry (which since January 1988 wishes to be recognized as 'The Department for Enterprise').

Throughout the 1980s there has, too, been a general shift in public attitudes, so that increasingly those who start and run a business are looked upon in a more favourable light. There has, in effect, been a revival of entrepreneurship in Britain and many entrepreneurs are now well-known figures; for example:

Alan Sugar, who started Amstrad, the consumer electronics firm
Richard Branson, the founder of Virgin
Anita Roddick, the co-founder of Body Shop
Terence Conran, who founded Habitat and now leads the Store-house group
Robert Maxwell, founder of Maxwell Communications Corporation.

There are many more lesser known entrepreneurs who have also been highly successful; for example:

Gerald Ratner, chief executive of Ratners, Britain's largest jewellery group

What it takes to make it – from those who have!

Achiever News, a mouthpiece of nationally based scheme Young Enterprise, approached well-known achievers in the world of business, entertainment, politics and other fields and asked them: 'What does it take to make it?'

10 DOWNING STREET

● **Margaret Thatcher – Prime Minister:**
'My best advice is to believe that your position in life will depend to a large extent on the amount of effort you are prepared to put into it. Everybody can't reach the top. But if you have the will, you can find a way to get the most from talents that you are blessed with. Take a step at a time and you will usually find there is another one ahead if you wish to take it.'

● **John Egan – Chairman and Chief Executive, Jaguar Daimler**
'Business is about making money out of satisfying customers – and big business is about harnessing the talents and enthusiasm of larger groups of people to the common purpose of creating products that satisfy customers.'

● **Ann Vinton – Founder of the Reject Shops**
'There are a lot of knocks, but you have to dust yourself down and come back fighting.'

● **Lord Patrick Litchfield – Royal photographer, entrepreneur**
'Look at the excellence in others and set yourself a goal to aspire to. Never ever settle for second best.'

● **Arthur Daley – Small-time businessman, alias George Cole:**
'You can do it, my son!'

● **Richard Branson – Chairman of the Virgin Group**
'Never take no for an answer. Even if the group outcome looks bleak, never lie down and die until you're dead'

● **Jennifer D'Abo – Chairman of Ryman Limited**
'To succeed you need determination, single-mindedness and the ability to grasp opportunities when they arise.'

● **Sir Terence Beckett – Director General, Confederation of British Industry:**
'Awareness, realism, dedication, maintenance of aim, enthusiasm. Look after the other person, friendship.'

● **Lord Charles Forte – Chairman, Trusthouse Forte Group**
'Success in business is never to sit back and assume you have achieved it. First get the right idea, second raise the adequate finance . . . and then work, work, work.'

● **Dr. Leah Hertz – Authoress and Businesswoman:**
'You need:
– a burning wish to succeed
– a pride in being different
– a desire to be a boss
– a realisation that success is 90% hard work and tenacity, and only 10% talent.'

● **Martyn Lewis – Journalist and TV Newsreader**
'Even when you're really down and you feel the whole world is against you, never give up. Sooner or later things will bounce back your way.'

Nigel Rudd, who runs William Holdings, a growing industrial conglomerate
John Ashcroft, who leads the Coloroll group, which designs and produces wallpapers and curtains.

Profiles of some of these entrepreneurs, and others, appear later in this book. It should be stressed that these profiles do not represent examples of particular theories; they are simply included as types of people who have behaved in an entrepreneurial manner. The extent to which any of them conform to the theories of the entrepreneur proposed by economists is left to the reader to decide.

It is interesting to note that many successful British entrepreneurs do not have a degree qualification. Alan Sugar, for example, left school in the East End of London to begin work at 16; Richard Branson left Stowe School to start his first major venture, the running of a magazine for students, when he was 17. Sir Clive Sinclair left St George's College at Weybridge at 17. Other notable entrepreneurs similarly have had no formal higher education, including Sir James Goldsmith, Lord Forte, Lord Hanson, Sir Terence Conran, Sir Philip Harris and Robert Maxwell.

This is not to suggest that such individuals could not have succeeded in obtaining a degree. Rather it is to emphasize the point that entrepreneurs often take the personal decision to end their formal education relatively early in order to learn how to establish and run a business; in effect they serve an apprenticeship as an entrepreneur. Perhaps this trend will change in the future as more new graduates take the decision not to become an employee but to become an entrepreneur. This is perhaps to be expected as many institutions of higher education are now running graduate enterprise programmes designed to help graduates set up small businesses. Whether or not the education system as a whole promotes entrepreneurship is subject to great dispute. The government has often taken the view that schools and colleges tend to discourage rather than encourage careers in business. This view is supported by Sir Nicholas Goodison, the former Chairman of the Stock Exchange. Read the accompanying article from *The Times* of 4 April 1986 by Philip Howard.

Lesson in classic economics

By Philip Howard

In his presidential address to the Classical Association of Scotland and England in Glasgow, Sir Nicholas Goodison, chairman of the Stock Exchange, scolded the British educational system for its attitude towards industry.

He asked whether enough is done in schools and universities to equip students of the humanities for life in a struggling economy. It was a question expecting the answer no. And it got it.

Sir Nicholas was saddened that the cultural tradition in Britain was strongly biased against trade and industry. He thought that the snobbish Edwardian put-down, "his family is in trade", still ruled.

In the country of Watt and Brunel, it was incredible that industrial management and engineering should be held in such low esteem by young people.

Britain could not succeed and prosper he said, unless the brightest and best were involved in industry. He had many suggestions to improve attitudes, including making business studies an important part of the humanities curriculum, industrial case studies replacing cadet corps field days and a basic business course for everybody.

Defining the entrepreneur

The term 'entrepreneur' is a word of French origin meaning one who undertakes a project, a contractor or master builder. It first made a significant appearance in the writing of Richard Cantillon, an eighteenth century businessman and financier. Cantillon's view of the entrepreneur is discussed in Chapter 3.

During the eighteenth century there were three commonly used English equivalents of the French term – these were 'adventurer', 'projector' and 'undertaker', with the latter becoming the more commonly used. At first 'undertaker' simply meant someone who set out to do a job or complete a project. Over time the term came to designate someone involved in a risky project from which an uncertain profit might be derived. Adam Smith in *The Wealth of Nations* regarded the undertaker as a capitalist and did not discuss the undertaker in terms of the entrepreneurial function. Partly because of the example provided by Smith the term undertaker eventually came to be replaced by the term capitalist, and during the nineteenth century 'undertaker' acquired the special meaning of an arranger of funerals that it has today.

Although it is possible to identify a number of individuals and claim that they are entrepreneurs, economists have found it rather more difficult to determine what an entrepreneur is and what it is that they do. Indeed there is a great deal of debate among economists about the meaning of entrepreneurship and just who, or what, is an entrepreneur. Entrepreneurship has been described by the economist S.M. Kanbur as 'the phenomenon which is most emphasized yet least understood by economists'.

As economics does not have a single view of who the entrepreneur is

5

or what the entrepreneur does, then clearly the elusive nature of the entrepreneur makes it difficult to arrive at a definition. There are, in fact, almost as many definitions of entrepreneurship as there are writers about entrepreneurs. The entrepreneur has been defined in all of the following ways:

1 The person who assumes the risk associated with uncertainty.
2 A decision-maker.
3 An innovator.
4 An industrial leader.
5 An organizer or coordinator of economic resources.
6 A contractor.
7 An arbitrageur.
8 The person who allocates resources to alternative uses.
9 A supplier of financial capital.
10 A manager or superintendent.
11 A proprietor of an enterprise.
12 An employer of factors of production.

This list is not exhaustive but indicates the differing ways in which the entrepreneur has been viewed by economists. Clearly some of the concepts overlap and the list does not necessarily imply that there are at least twelve different theories of the entrepreneur. It is possible, in fact, to allocate these twelve notions to three distinctive types of theory about the entrepreneur. Before doing so, however, it is necessary to distinguish between **static** and **dynamic views** of the economy.

In a *static* world nothing would change and there would be no uncertainty. In such an economy the entrepreneur's role would be no more than is implied in the final four items (9, 10, 11 or 12) listed above. The entrepreneur would, at best, simply be a passive element with his actions merely being repetitions of past procedures and the implementation of well-known techniques. In a *dynamic* world, however, one in which there is change and uncertainty, the entrepreneur has an active role. The entrepreneur is no longer concerned merely with perpetuating the existing state of affairs but with improving upon it; the entrepreneur becomes an agent of change. A dynamic framework therefore gives support for entrepreneurial action implied by the first eight items. It is further possible to allocate these items to three basic types of entrepreneurial theory, and an outline of the way economists have viewed the entrepreneurial function in a dynamic framework, and their main areas of disagreement, now follows.

Risk and uncertainty (items 1 and 2)

Historically, the **risk-bearing** function of entrepreneurship was stressed first. As already noted, the term 'entrepreneur' first made a significant appearance in the writing of Richard Cantillon, who argued that he or she was someone who has the foresight and willingness to assume risk and take the action required to make a profit.

The risk-bearing function became less important in the discussion of entrepreneurship after the establishment of **limited liability** (where the liability of a company's shareholders is limited to the amount they have agreed to subscribe to the capital of the company) and the associated new forms of business organization, such as the joint stock company. However, the function of the entrepreneur shouldering the burden of the risks arising from uncertainty was re-emphasized earlier this century by Frank Knight in his examination of the returns to the entrepreneur in the form of profit.

While the risk-bearing function is often stressed in the economic analysis of the entrepreneur, in contrast Joseph Schumpeter and other economists have argued that risking one's financial capital is not intrinsic to the entrepreneurial function but that this is instead the role of the capitalist.

Innovation (items 3, 4, 5 and 6)

A second major development emphasized **innovation** more than other aspects of entrepreneurship. This view is particularly associated with Schumpeter's classic definition of the entrepreneur as the person who creates 'new combinations' in the production and distribution of goods and services. According to Schumpeter a person is an entrepreneur only when he or she is engaged in innovative behaviour, which constitutes the entrepreneurial function. Moreover, this activity will lead to *disequilibrium* in markets.

Perception and adjustment (items 7 and 8)

A third wave of entrepreneurial theories in turn stressed the importance of **perception** and **adjustment**. Basically, it is argued that it is the actions of the entrepreneur reacting to price movements – and hence profit opportunities – that continually serve to bring about a balance between supplies and demands in specific markets. In effect the entrepreneur acts as a mechanism to produce *equilibrium* in a market economy. This view of the entrepreneur is particularly associated with the Austrian school of economics.

There is clearly a diversity of views over the role of the entrepreneur. There is also disagreement over the context in which entrepreneurship occurs. Some writers argue that it can exist only in small businesses and tend to take the view that large companies inhibit the exercise of entrepreneurship (for example, because of the lack of autonomy and control an individual is able to exercise, and the apparent lack of financial risk). In contrast other writers have stressed recently that entrepreneurship can be found in large as well as small businesses, introducing the term 'intrapreneurship' to describe entrepreneurial activity in large organizations. These debates over the meaning and location of entrepreneurship are likely to persist.

The main ways in which economists have viewed the entrepreneur will be examined in rather more detail in later chapters. The following chapter examines the somewhat surprising treatment of the entrepreneur in standard economic theory.

KEY WORDS

Entrepreneurship	Limited liability
Static view	Innovation
Dynamic view	Perception
Risk-bearing	Adjustment

Essay topics

1. 'You can't make entrepreneurs but the education system can destroy them' (Lord Young). Discuss this view.
2. 'Entrepreneurship is difficult to define but easy to recognize.' Discuss.
3. Distinguish between a static and a dynamic economic environment. What role is there for an entrepreneur in a static world?

Reading list

Glaister, K.W., 'The entrepreneur: enigma of economic theory', *Economics: The Journal of the Economics Association*, Vol. XXIV, Part 1, No. 101, Spring 1988.

Heathfield, D., *Modern Economics*, Philip Allan, 1987, pp. 37, 40, 42–50.

Lipsey, R. and Harbury, C., *First Principles of Economics*, Weidenfeld & Nicolson, 1988, p. 6.

Maunders, P., Myers, D. and Wall, N., *Economics Explained*, Collins Educational, 1988, p. 3.

Powell, R., *A-Level Economics Course Companion*, Letts, 3rd edn, 1988, p. 38.

Stanlake, G.R., *Introductory Economics*, 4th edn, Longman, 1983, pp. 14, 37–8, 51.

Data Response Question 1

British Social Attitudes Survey

Read the accompanying article from the *Financial Times* of 3 November 1988, which discusses the fifth report of the Survey, *Social and Community Planning Research,* published by Gower Publishing. Answer the following questions.

1. What do you understand by the terms (a) 'enterprise culture' and (b) 'dependency culture'?
2. What are 'the fruits of business investment and entrepreneurship'? Who receives such 'fruits' and who do you think *ought* to receive them?
3. What are the goals of the enterprise culture?
4. Should the government cut tax rates to encourage business investment and entrepreneurship if the reduction in tax revenue means that less can be spent on hospitals, education and the social services? Justify your view.

Support for 'enterprise culture' dwindles

Public opinion has become less sympathetic during the 1980s to central elements of the Government's attempt to transform Britain into an "enterprise culture," the latest British Social Attitudes Survey suggests today.

The survey casts doubt on the extent to which Mrs Margaret Thatcher, the prime Minister, has succeeded since 1979 in moving the nation from a "dependency culture" to one embodying "rewards for individual effort, entrepreneurship and the assumption of responsibility, and disapproval of reliance on the state."

It says Mrs Thatcher set herself the revolutionary task of reforming not only institutions and their practices but British culture itself. If she had succeeded, it continues, the public would regard the fruits of business investment and entrepreneurship as a legitimate reward for shareholders and top managers. People would support cuts in social expenditure and

9

the progressive privatisation of health and education, and would frown on Keynesian solutions to unemployment such as job creation.

Yet the compilers of the survey say there is evidence that, "despite all the exhortations over the last eight years," such views are embraced by only a minority of the public. Since 1983 when the Social Attitudes Survey began, public opinion has actually become more allienated from many of the goals of the enterprise culture, they say.

They add: "To the extent that attitudes have moved, they have become less sympathetic to these central tenets of the Thatcher revolution."

Their report accepts that it takes time to change a political culture and that the shift may still occur. It identifies as a serious obstacle to change the faint-heartedness of many people who should be in the vanguard of promoting the new culture.

They are unconvinced, for instance, that industrial profits should go primarily to entrepreneurs or shareholders or top managers, being generally sympathetic to the claims of workers and customers."

The Social Attitudes Survey is sponsored by government, charitable and private sources. One example of growing support for public spending is contained in its results on attitudes towards the National Health Service.

Although levels of general dissatisfaction with the NHS have increased – from 25 per cent in 1983 to nearly 40 per cent last year – support for the principle of state health care, and increased public expenditure to provide it, has grown stronger during the same period.

Although the debate about the future of health care is often presented in terms of greater private spending, the report says, the survey shows that the public does not see the question in those terms.

There had been little change in the public's view of the private sector. But the proportion of survey respondents who regard health as the first or second priority for increased public spending has risen from 63 per cent in 1983 to 79 per cent last year.

Variations in attitudes between the north and south of Britain cannot be explained entirely by differences in the economic and employment status of the people who live there, the survey report states.

Even when differences in class, tenure and work status have been taken into account, people in the north are more likely to have egalitarian views and negative expectations about the economy than those in the south.

The report says the north's greater egalitarian preferences cannot be explained solely by its higher level of identification with the Labour Party.

In terms of variations in attitudes, the survey draws the north-south dividing line from the Mersey to the Humber and along Offa's Dyke. Region, the survey says, now accompanies class as a basis of voting behaviour and as an influence on social attitudes, although it has not replaced it.

Alan Pike

Social Affairs Correspondent

Data Response Question 2

Victorian industrialists

Read the accompanying article from the *Times* which discusses Ian Bradley's book *Englightened Entrepreneurs*, and answer the following questions.

1. In your view is the entrepreneur an esteemed figure in modern Britain?
2. Do you think that modern entrepreneurs are less concerned for the social and physical welfare of their employees than were the entrepreneurs of 100 years ago? Justify your view.

Ian Bradley finds an example for today's tycoon in the concern and moral vision of the great Victorian industrialists

Despite the efforts made to change popular attitudes in Britain towards industry, the entrepreneur is still far from being an esteemed figure. I suspect that one main reason is that most reports we read about successful businessmen have the character of scandals rather than romances. The Guinness affair has confirmed a picture already well formed in the national consciousness.

However, even allowing for the fact that the media highlight human weakness, the popular perception of entrepreneurs as sharp-dealing, fast-living jet-setters who are not much concerned for the general welfare is understandable. The image that some leading industrialists and tycoons project through their lifestyles and attitudes is not exactly heroic.

This is in marked contrast with the situation 100 years ago, when many British industrialists were generally regarded not just as heroes but almost as saints – with some reason, given the nature of their attitudes and achievements. I have just finished a study of 10 of the most successful British industrialists in the 19th century, among them the men who founded or built up such companies as Cadburys, Rowntrees, Boots, Reckitt and Colman and Unilever. All of them became very rich, but they also all developed into political radicals, generous philanthropists and remarkably enlightened employers.

The Victorian values they espoused were more complex and humane than those to which Mrs Thatcher and others would have us return. They are worth studying and even copying by modern-day entrepreneurs, who might envy and wonder at the esteem in which they were held.

It is true that the Thatcherite themes of self-help, thrift and hard work were dominant features in the lives of these Victorian and Edwardian entrepreneurs. All of them came from comparatively humble origins and not one of them went to university.

One of the most striking features of this remarkably successful group of entrepreneurs was that they did not allow their increasing wealth to change their habits or lifestyle. They continued to take pride in being in their factories before most of their workers, often having begun the day with a bracing cold bath or shower, and they were usually still at their desks long after the workforce had gone home. Social engagements were largely shunned in favour of domestic recreations of a strikingly wholesome and sober kind. Of the 10 entrepreneurs in my study – and there were many more like them – seven were teetotal and the other three drank very little.

Perhaps more important, from the point of view of their workforce, they remained essentially provincial figures, resisting the lure of London and preferring to keep their offices close to their factories. They also continued to live near their employees rather than retreating to expensive and isolated mansions in the country. Within their works they were accessible to employees.

Concern for the social and physical welfare of employees inspired the model industrial communities of Saltaire near Bradford, Bournville in Birmingham, New Earswick in York and Port Sunlight on the Wirral, which stand today as attractive living memorials to the enlightened face of Victorian capitalism, even if now they are largely gentrified and likely to be lived in by middle-class commuters.

In these communities Titus Salt, the richest and most powerful of the West Yorkshire textile barons who employed more than 3,500 in his worsted mills, George Cadbury, Joseph Rowntree and William Lever pioneered the garden city idea and introduced many revolutionary principles of urban housing and design. Others led the way in different areas of social welfare, such as the occupational health service provided by Jeremiah Colman in his Norwich mustard works.

Of course, circumstances have changed considerably. The climate in which British industry operates is much less favourable than it was in the heyday of our commercial supremacy. Competition is more intense, the need to cut costs more pressing, and there is an extensive state welfare system to provide many of the benefits that were offered by enlightened Victorian employers. Paternalism is out of fashion with unions and with management. Lines of communications at all levels of business and industry tend to be official rather than personal. But even allowing for all this it is hard to avoid the conclusion that today's entrepreneurs are a different breed, and that is why they command so much less respect.

How many modern industrialists could say, as Joseph Rowntree did with all sincerity in the first issue of his *Cocoa Works Magazine*, that their aim in life was that of "combining social progress with commercial success"?

In Victorian times business was seen as a romance and books by the score portrayed the lives of entrepreneurs both as gripping adventure stories and also as examples of high moral principle, dedication to public service and concern for others. Is it too much to hope that modern entrepreneurs might provide the material for such romances today, rather than just more subject matter for the modern equivalents of the penny dreadfuls?

Chapter Two

The entrepreneur in standard economic theory

Once the initial decision has been taken to maximize some objective function . . . the decision-making process reduces to that of a calculating robot.

The central problem that mainstream economic thought (i.e. neoclassical analysis) has focused on is that of understanding how a decentralized economic system allocates resources. Basically, this involves an analysis of the coordinating role of prices to produce a **general equilibrium** outcome, where each market in the economy is in equilibrium simultaneously. Resource allocation thus involves consideration of the three fundamental problems of economic organization:

- *What* goods and services should be produced and in what quantities?
- *How* should goods be produced? In other words by whom should goods be produced, with what resources and what technology?
- *For whom* should goods be produced? That is, how should the total of national output be distributed?

Under a competitive **free enterprise** system no individual or organization consciously sets out to solve those three fundamental questions. A competitive enterprise system does, however, provide an automatic mechanism for coordination of resource allocations through a system of prices and markets. Essentially the 'what', 'how' and 'for whom' questions are resolved by the operation of buyers and sellers responding to price signals in markets for goods and services.

The invisible hand

That a free enterprise system would lead to a decentralized allocation of resources through the operation of prices and markets was first discussed by Adam Smith in his major work *The Wealth of Nations*, published in 1776. Smith likened the coordinating role of the market to the working of an '**invisible hand**'. The key idea is found in the following quotation from Book IV, Chapter 2:

'But it is only for the sake of profit that any man employs his capital in the support of industry, and he always will, therefore, endeavour to employ it in the support of that industry of which the produce is likely to be of the greatest value, or to exchange for the greatest quantity either of money or other goods . . .. He is in this, as in many other cases, led by an invisible hand to promote an end which was no part of his intention. Nor is it always the worse for the society that it was no part of it. By pursuing his own interest he frequently promotes that of the society more effectively than when he really intends to promote it.'

The essential idea is that each person will be motivated by rational self-interest to use the resources they have wherever the highest possible price may be obtained. High prices reflect scarcity of supply compared with the strength of consumers' demands. Self-interest will therefore work continuously to overcome scarcity and meet consumer demands, and in this way resources will be directed to those uses most suited for satisfying consumer demand. Adam Smith argued that every individual, by pursuing his or her own self-interest, would respond effectively to market opportunities and would thus be led, as if by an invisible hand, to achieve the best, or optimum, situation for society as a whole.

The assumption of perfect competition
Smith's insight of the invisible hand and the way in which a free enterprise market system would lead to an **optimum allocation** of resources was studied in detail by later economists. It was eventually established that if every market in the economy is a perfectly competitive free market, the resulting equilibrium throughout the economy would be what is termed '**Pareto-efficient**' (from the early twentieth century economist Vilfredo Pareto). An allocation is Pareto-efficient if it is impossible to move to a different allocation which would make some people better off without making others worse off. A Pareto-efficient allocation thus means that nobody can be made better off without making someone else worse off.

Although the operation of a free market system will lead to the attainment of a general equilibrium, mainstream economists stressed that only if **perfect competition** is assumed to exist in both product markets (the markets for goods and services) and factor markets (the markets for resources such as labour, land and capital) will the resulting general equilibrium also be Pareto-efficient. Because economists were concerned to show that, if left to itself, a free market economy would produce an equilibrium outcome which could not be improved upon – in the Pareto-efficient sense – they tended to stress economic models that assumed perfect competition. The assumption that every market in the economy operated under conditions of perfect competition had significant implications for the way in which the entrepreneur was treated within the theory of the firm. It may be argued, in fact, that the theoretical firm of the perfectly competitive model is 'entrepreneurless'!

Under the assumptions of perfect competition the firm is a **price taker**; that is, decisions of the firm will be based on prevailing market prices which the individual firm cannot affect. For a given market price, and with knowledge of its costs, the main problem for the firm is to decide on an output level which will maximize profit – the firm acts as a **profit maximizer**. The firm is required to make a mathematical calculation – the equating of **marginal revenue** and **marginal cost** – which gives the optimum value for the firm's output level, in that this is the output level at which the firm will maximize profits. This, in effect, constitutes the business decision of the firm. Correct decision-making in this non-entrepreneurial sense means correct calculation, and faulty decision-making is equivalent to mistakes in arithmetic.

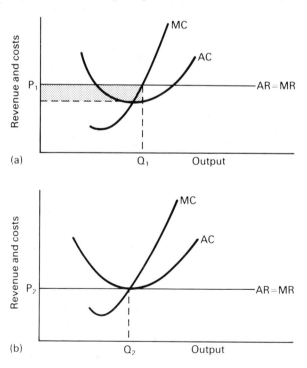

Figure 1   The firm in perfect competition: (a) short-run equilibrium and (b) long-run equilibrium

Figure 1 shows the equilibrium of a firm in perfect competition. In (a) the firm equates marginal cost with marginal revenue to obtain the profit-maximizing output level Q_1. The firm will earn abnormal profit in the short run as average revenue exceeds average cost. The total amount of abnormal profit earned is shown by the shaded area. New firms will be attracted into the market by the prospect of earning abnormal profit. The total supply to the market will increase, causing the market price to fall. This process will continue until all firms in the market are earning only normal profit. For the individual firm this situation is shown in (b). Now the firm equates marginal cost and marginal revenue to obtain the profit-maximizing level of output Q_2. At this output level the average revenue is at the same level as the average cost, and so the firm is earning only normal profit.

Once the profit-maximizing output level has been decided on the firm is assumed to be in **equilibrium**, and there will be no tendency to change this decision. The firm is thus assumed to repeat its previous decisions consistently through time. The only reason for the decision to be changed is if market conditions change: for example if the market price changes, or costs of factor inputs change. The firm will then recalculate on the basis of the change imposed on the firm, again seeking a profit-maximizing value for its output level.

In such a model of the firm there is no role for the entrepreneur. The decision-making body of the firm is essentially composed of a management group which is a passive calculator that reacts mechanically to changes imposed on it by external developments over which it has no control and does not attempt to influence. Moreover, there is no room for enterprise or initiative. As Baumol puts it:

'One hears of no clever ruses, ingenious schemes, brilliant innovations, of no charisma or any of the other stuff of which outstanding entrepreneurship is made; one does not hear of them because there is no way in which they can fit into the model'.

In the standard economic model of perfect competition, therefore, the firm acts as an automaton maximizer: there is no entrepreneur.

Alternative models

Of course, mainstream economists have developed models of the firm that do not rely on the assumptions of perfect competition. Models have been developed, for instance, which analyse the firm in situations of monopoly (where there is only one supplier) or imperfect competition (where there may be a large number of firms but each has distinctive or differentiated products). Such models assume, however, that the firm has a single objective, that of profit maximization. Hence the decision-making process within the firm again becomes that of mechanically equating marginal revenue and marginal cost to obtain the optimum output level. The essence of the decision-making process within the firm is the same as for the model of perfect competition, and again there is no role for the entrepreneur.

It is also the case that mainstream economists have developed models of the firm which assume that the firm has an objective other than profit maximization. For example, the firm may be assumed to maximize its sales revenue or its rate of growth. It would appear, however, that these models of the firm are no improvement on the model of the firm in perfect competition when considering the entrepreneur. Once the initial decision has been taken to maximize some **objective function**, then the decision-making process within the firm, as in the case of profit maximization, reduces to that of a calculating robot. The management group will make and enforce the maximizing decision, and thus the choice of objective to be maximized makes no difference to the essential way in which the outcome is reached. It is based on a mere mathematical calculation. The decision characteristics of the firm are thus mechanistic and automatic and they call for no display of entrepreneurial initiative.

Conclusions

The model of the firm in standard economic theory was developed in a way which assumed that it operated like a predictable, impersonal and frictionless machine. There is no role for the entrepreneur in such a model: the standard theory of the firm is thus 'entrepreneurless' or an 'inhuman model'. In contrast, the world of real firms is inhabited by individuals of ambition who seek to alter their economic environment and not merely to respond to it. Although the standard model of the firm if a useful analytical device and performs an important role in the understanding of how the decentralized allocation of resources may produce a Pareto-efficient general equilibrium, on its own it is a purely mechanistic model which says nothing about entrepreneurial activity.

The standard model assumes that decision-making within the firm is based on objective and completely certain figures of costs and revenues. The data on which the real-world entrepreneur has to make decisions is, though, not objective. The entrepreneur has to decide *in advance* what revenue and costs will be, and his or her ideas about them are therefore subjective estimates which will incorporate the entrepreneur's own beliefs and guesses. The entrepreneur may miscalculate, however, in which case the beliefs and guesses may turn out to be incorrect. The best that a profit-maximizing entrepreneur can do is to equate his *estimate* of marginal cost with his *estimate* of marginal revenue. The entrepreneur can never be quite certain in advance what either marginal cost or marginal revenue will actually turn out to be. This realization brings us to the notion that the entrepreneur is in fact a risk-taker in the sense that such a person must contend with uncertainties. The theories which examine the entrepreneur in this light are considered in the next chapter.

KEY WORDS

General equilibrium	Price taker
Free enterprise	Profit maximizer
Invisible hand	Marginal revenue
Optimum allocation	Marginal cost
Pareto-efficient	Equilibrium
Perfect competition	Objective function

Essay topics
1. 'There is no role for the entrepreneur in the perfectly competitive firm.' Explain this statement.
2. 'Models which assume that the firm seeks to maximize profit, or sales, or growth, leave no room for the role of the entrepreneur.' What is the basis for this view and do you agree with it?

Reading list
Glaister, K.W., 'The entrepreneur: enigma of economic theory', *Economics: Journal of the Economics Association*, vol. XXIV, part 1, Spring 1988.
Heathfield, D., *Modern Economics*, Philip Allan, 1987, pp. 37, 40, 42–50.

Chapter Three

The entrepreneur, risk and uncertainty

'The fact is that one side thinks that the profits to be won outweigh the risks to be incurred.' Thucydides

In order that economic activity may take place, someone must organize the **factors of production**. In other words someone must combine the factor inputs of **labour, land** and **capital** in such a way that consumer demands may be met. The role of organization may be regarded, however, as a managerial function which can be performed by a paid manager. The person who undertakes this role of coordination and organization – that is, 'management' – should be classified, therefore, under the 'labour' heading as the management are in effect the paid employees of the firm. Viewing the organization role in this way leaves the distinguishing feature of entrepreneurship that of **risk-bearing**, with the receipt of **profit** being seen as the reward for taking the risks of business.

Of course, it is not always easy to separate the function of the entrepreneur from that of the manager; indeed, in many small businesses a single individual will not only manage the firm but also undertake the entrepreneurial role. However, where the function of the entrepreneur is to bear risk, the managerial tasks of organizing and coordinating factor inputs as effectively as possible are not seen as part of the true entrepreneurial function. According to this view the true entrepreneur is the person who risks losses and earns pure profit: it is not necessary that the entrepreneur should coordinate and manage factors of production at all.

Richard Cantillon's view of the entrepreneur
The notion of the entrepreneur as a risk-bearer was recognized relatively early in the study of entrepreneurship by an Irishman, Richard Cantillon, a businessman and financier. Cantillon's *Essay on the Nature of Commerce* was first published in 1755, 21 years after the author's death. His was the first important work in economics that gave the entrepreneur a central role in trade. Cantillon showed the entrepreneur to be a pivotal figure who operates within a set of economic markets. For Cantillon the entrepreneur had a central role in

bringing about equilibrium prices in markets and in this respect Cantillon's work is very close to some modern views of the entrepreneur.

Cantillon stressed, however, that an entrepreneur is someone who has both the foresight and the willingness to assume risk and take the necessary action required to making a profit (or bearing a loss). He pointed out that some people – for example, craftsmen, wholesalers, retailers, innkeepers, tailors and others – buy at a certain price and sell at an uncertain price. They thus operate at risk.

Cantillon argued that the origin of entrepreneurship lies in the lack of foresight individuals have with regard to the future. For Cantillon, uncertainty was a pervasive fact of everyday life and those who must deal with it continuously in their economic pursuits are entrepreneurs. The first formal statement of the entrepreneur's role and significance in the market economy was provided by Cantillon, who also developed one of the most enduring concepts of the entrepreneur.

Cantillon's explanation of the entrepreneur's role has a supply side emphasis. It views the entrepreneur as providing the right goods at the right place in order to satisfy given consumer wishes. He does not see the entrepreneur as creating demand through new production developments or by marketing techniques. Thus, although Cantillon's entrepreneurs must be forward-looking, they need not be innovative in the sense of creating anything new. The entrepreneur must be alert to profit opportunities, however, and these opportunities will occur when demand and supply do not match in particular markets.

Uncertainty and profit

The modern view that the entrepreneur is basically a risk-bearer and that the profit is the reward for risk-bearing stems from the work of the American economist Frank Knight, who first published his ideas in *Risk, Uncertainty and Profit* in 1921. Knight's important contribution was to emphasize the distinction between insurable risks and non-insurable uncertainty and to develop a theory of profit that related to this non-insurable uncertainty.

Knight argued that previous 'risk theories' were ambiguous because they did not distinguish sufficiently between two very different kinds of risk. On the one hand, risk means a quantity capable of being measured; in other words, the objective probability that an event will happen. However, because this kind of risk can be shifted from the entrepreneur to another party by an insurance contract, it is not an **uncertainty** in any meaningful sense. On the other hand, 'risk' is often taken to mean an unmeasurable unknown, such as the inability to predict consumer demand. Knight termed the latter 'true' uncertainty and geared his theories of profit and entrepreneurship to its magnitude. Knight's work offered a new refinement to Cantillon's theory of the entrepreneur as the bearer of uncertainty because it isolated the concept of uncertainty and sharpened its meaning. The nature of risks facing an entrepreneur is discussed more fully in the following section.

The nature of risks

Some of the risks a firm faces are calculable, in the sense that a statistician is able to calculate the likelihood, or the probability, of the event occurring. It is thus possible to calculate, for a particular firm in a particular location, the probability that it will suffer losses from such events as fire, theft, storm damage, accidents to employees or the death of the managing director. Because such risks can be calculated, however, it is possible for the firm to be insured against them. In other words, where the laws of probability may be applied to an event this allows the degree of risk to be calculated accurately, and hence an insurance may be taken out against loss should the event actually occur.

The entrepreneur, not wishing to deliberately take risks which can be avoided, is able to shift the burden of, for example, fire risk to the insurance company by paying the insurance premium. The fire insurance premium, as are insurance premiums for other calculable risks, is a cost of production, in the same way that wage payments or interest payments on loans are. So by paying a premium to an insurance company such risks are reduced to a **normal cost** and the firm is able to contract out of the risks involved. If the event does occur, the firm will be compensated by the insurance company for the loss.

There are certain other kinds of risks, though, which are not amenable to calculation because it is not possible to estimate the probability of the event occurring. As Frank Knight put it: 'Situations in regard to which business judgement must be exercised do not repeat themselves with sufficient uniformity to type to make possible a computation of probability.' For instance, the risk of the demand for a product being different from that estimated cannot be reduced to a statistical probability. Such a risk, therefore, cannot be insured against and consequently must be accepted by the entrepreneur.

It is thus impossible for the entrepreneur to insure against commercial losses or business failure. Although it is possible for an insurance company to estimate accurately the percentage of all firms which will have a fire in a year, it is not possible to say what percentage of firms in an industry will suffer a commercial loss, or what the level of these losses will be. It is quite possible that all firms will make a profit or that all might experience a loss. As statisticians are unable to calculate the probability that a given group of firms will make profits or losses in any year, it is not possible for an insurance company to insure a firm against such a loss. The insurance company would not know what level of premium to charge in order that it could compensate all these loss-making firms, and there would be a grave danger, for example, in a recession, that so many firms would suffer losses that the insurance company itself would become bankrupt.

Uncertainty and the competitive environment

It should now be clear that entrepreneurs have to compete with each other in conditions of uncertainty, in that they must face non-insurable risks. The nature of these uncertainties means that the future is unknown, and so in taking decisions entrepreneurs must make judgements on how likely the outcome of their action will be. From the cost side of the firm's operations the entrepreneur must come to a view on what will happen in factor markets if the firm increases its demand for inputs following a higher level of demand for its own output. If the firm's demand for particular inputs is a large proportion of total demand, a significant increase in its factor requirements may raise factor prices, but in other circumstances factor prices may remain unchanged. It may also be possible that unit factor prices may fall if the firm is able to achieve pecuniary **economies of scale** as its output level expands. The entrepreneur must attempt to forecast the most likely situation. The entrepreneur will also have to estimate how costs that are directly under the firm's control will alter as ouput changes; for example, marketing costs and research and development costs, both of which may be difficult to estimate.

The general business environment

Even where an entrepreneur intends to leave the output level unchanged, future uncertainty means that it is still necessary for him to have a view on likely events: such as whether or not factor input prices are likely to change or whether there will be a significant change in technology which may make the firm's current capital stock less efficient than that of innovating competitors.

The entrepreneur also needs to consider to what extent the general business environment is likely to change, and if so with what implications for the firm's operations – for example whether it will become more difficult to raise new finance, either from shareholders or by loans from banks and other financial institutions, and to what extent this will constrain future expansion plans.

Marketing strategies

On the revenue side, the entrepreneur must estimate how customers will respond to marketing initiatives such as a price reduction, an advertising campaign or a new product launch. The entrepreneur has also to estimate what will happen if current marketing strategies remain unchanged. Thus he needs to estimate what will happen to product demand if, for example, prices remain unaltered, there is no change in advertising expenditure and there is no new product launch.

What will be particularly significant will be the entrepreneur's judgement of the likely behaviour of rivals and potential rivals – the entrepreneur must come to some view on what competitors are likely to do, in terms of pricing policy, advertising campaigns, etc., whether or not the entrepreneur changes any of these variables for his own firm.

The uncertainty of demand

A fundamental problem for the entrepreneur is that production is usually undertaken in **anticipation** of demand. Entrepreneurs will therefore seek to produce those goods and services which they believe will yield a profit, but entrepreneurs do not know that they will do so because the future is unknown. Moreover, production takes time. Decisions about what should be produced must be taken months or even years before the goods will actually appear on the market. At the present time plans are being put into operation to produce more cars, televisions, video recorders, washing machines, microwave ovens, refrigerators, etc., which will cost hundreds of millions of pounds and may not be completed for several years. These decisions are being taken in anticipation of demand; there is no certainty that consumers will wish to purchase all that has been produced.

Reducing the uncertainty

It may be possible, to an extent, to reduce the degree of uncertainty. An entrepreneur may, for example, obtain a good deal of information by undertaking market research in an attempt to assess the demand for a new product. A firm may undertake a pilot selling exercise of a new product in a particular region of the country to test consumer reaction before marketing the product nationally. To provide greater certainty on costs and prices a firm may seek long-term contracts with suppliers and customers.

It is not possible, however, for uncertainty over the future to be completely eliminated. An entrepreneur will not really know whether a particular strategy will work until it has actually been implemented.

Anticipated profit . . . actual loss

The entrepreneur must hire labour, invest in capital equipment and buy raw materials in order to produce goods which will not be sold until some time in the future. Whether the entrepreneur recovers the costs of production will depend on the level of demand *when the goods are available to sell*. From the time the decision to produce has been taken to the time the finished goods are available for consumption there may have been a change in tastes away from the good (consider, for example, the number of firms which were left with unsold stocks of skate-boards in the 1970s); or the entrepreneur may simply produce a product which consumers do not particularly want (for example, Sir Clive Sinclair's C5 electric car which was launched in 1985 but failed to find many buyers). Another danger is that a rival producer may, in the time it takes the product to come on to the market, be selling a substitute good at a lower price, which he is able to do because he has developed a more effective technical process. Under such circumstances an anticipated profit may turn out to be an actual loss.

Conclusions

A widely accepted theory of the entrepreneur is based on the view that entrepreneurs earn profit for facing the burden of decision-making under conditions of uncertainty. If there were never any changes in such things as the population level, individuals' tastes and preferences, the nature of technology or income levels, and if everyone knew that they would not change, or if they did change that the changes could be accurately predicted, then there would be no uncertainty. The demand for all goods and services could be met by existing firms which, having once adjusted their prices and output levels to the unchanging market situation, would continue indefinitely producing the same goods for the same group of consumers by the same methods. The real world, though, is dynamic and uncertain. The role of the entrepreneur, according to the tradition of Cantillon and Knight, is to shoulder the burden of this uncertainty.

KEY WORDS

Factors of production	Profit
Labour	Uncertainty
Land	Normal cost
Capital	Economies of scale
Risk-bearing	Anticipation

Essay topics

1. Distinguish between insurable risk and non-insurable uncertainty. Why must the entrepreneur shoulder the burden of uncertainty?
2. Identify the factors which produce uncertainty in the economic environment.
3. 'If the future is known with certainty then there is no role for the entrepreneur.' Discuss.

Reading list

Lipsey, R. and Harbury, C., *First Principles of Economics*, Weidenfeld & Nicolson, 1988, p. 6.

Maunders, P., Myers, D. and Wall, N., *Economics Explained*, Collins Educational, 1988, p.3.

Powell, R., *A-Level Economics Course Companion*, Letts, 3rd edn, 1988, p. 38.

Stanlake, G.R., *Introductory Economics*, 4th edn, Longman, 1983, pp. 14, 37–8, 51.

PROFILE: Richard Branson, founder of Virgin Group plc

Virgin originated in 1970 when Richard Branson established a business selling popular records by mail order. The first Virgin shop was opened in Oxford Street, London, in 1971. By the end of 1978, a record company, a music publishing company, a recording studio operation and an export company had been added. By the end of 1979, the Virgin record company had a growing presence in the UK and, predominantly on a licensing basis, in overseas markets.

While at boarding school in Stowe and still only 15, Branson established an international magazine for students, selling advertising over the school payphone. Branson eventually raised £4000 and left school at 17 to establish the magazine *Student* which he worked on for four years. He then started selling LPs by mail order. He chose 'Virgin' as the name for the company in order to reflect his innocence of the ways of business. Branson eventually established a record company. The first album released on the Virgin label was Mike Oldfield's *Tubular Bells*, which proved to be a huge success, selling millions of copies.

Branson runs Virgin from a houseboat on the Regent's Canal, delegating the day-to-day running of its outposts to his codirectors and to managing directors of the three core businesses – Music, Retail, and Property and Communications – who are allowed considerable autonomy. Observers have claimed that Branson has always run Virgin in the manner of a paternalistic Victorian mill-owner, encouraging employees to air grievances to him personally, rewarding them with generous bonuses and foreign holidays.

Branson has been described by critics as the archetypal 'hippy capitalist', summarized by his biographer Mick Brown as 'sowing the seeds of his fortune in a shrewd understanding of the mores and tastes of a hazy era of libertarian-idealism, and reaping the fruits in an era of pragmatic commercialism'. Brown argues that it is probably the case that Branson has always equally enjoyed eschewing convention and making money. Colleagues from his days with *Student* apparently remember him as 'a public-school Arthur Daley' with a perennial eye for the half-chance.

In November 1986, the Virgin Group was floated on the stockmarket at a price of 140p per share, valuing the company at about £250 million. At the time of the flotation Branson's declared aim was to make Virgin a £1 billion company within five years, with the long-term aim of making it 'the greatest entertainment business in the world'.

Not all of the leisure and entertainment activities associated with Branson were included in the flotation. In particular Virgin Atlantic Airlines, plus associated small freight and holiday tour-operating businesses and Branson's London nightclubs and discotheques, were stripped out of the group and injected into a new private company named Voyager, of which Branson is chairman. It was believed that income from these activities was too volatile, and that investors' confidence in Virgin Atlantic would be troubled by fears of terrorism and its deterrent effect on tourist travellers, such that if they were included in the Virgin Group they might damage the success of the public flotation.

Although Branson's well-publicized dare-devil crossings of the Atlantic have earned him something of a reputation as a reckless individual, he in fact has a very sensible attitude towards risk in business. Branson has said that 'limiting the downside' is his overriding concern, which in effect means minimizing the risk of loss in any business venture. On the retail side, for example, Virgin ensure that their leases or freeholds are easily realizable so that they are not trapped into loss-making shops. This rule proved useful in mid-1988 when Virgin sold its 74 small record shops, which produced poor profit figures, to the Our Price retail chain.

Following the flotation of Virgin the share price performed relatively poorly. Shortly after its launch at 140p it reached a peak of 177p, subsequently falling to a low of 83p. Virgin shares were not particularly liked by the major institutional investors such as the pension funds and life insurance companies, none of which had a major shareholding in the Virgin Group. Exasperated by the City's lack of understanding of the company, Branson made the company private again by buying the Virgin shares back in a management buyout in January 1989. It is believed that Branson will be happier tending his business privately without having to justify his plans to City brokers and institutions. With the Virgin Group under private control, it is again run alongside the airline, which ironically has proved the most profitable part of Branson's empire.

Branson is always considering the future direction of the Virgin Group. New ventures are his major interest – once a project is up and running he delegates responsibility to others. 'I like getting my teeth into new challenges. I like making things work when others are sceptical, and surprising the pundits' – Richard Branson (quoted in *Management Today*, March 1988).

Chapter Four

The entrepreneur and innovation

The carrying out of new combinations we call "enterprise"; the individuals whose function is to carry them out we call "entrepreneurs",' J.A. Schumpeter

A significant change of emphasis regarding the role of the entrepreneur came about from the writings of Joseph Schumpeter (1883-1950), who stressed the relationship between entrepreneurship and innovation. According to Schumpeter a person is an entrepreneur only when he or she is engaged in innovative behaviour, which constitutes the entrepreneurial function. Moreover, this activity will lead to disequilibrium in markets.

Schumpeter and the process of innovation
Schumpeter identified three phases in the process of technical change: namely, **invention**, **innovation** and **diffusion**.

Invention
An invention is the creation of *any* new idea and so the term is not only restricted to advances in science and technology. Thus, although it is usual to think of invention as the creation of a new product involving scientific advance (for example, the invention of the compact disc player) or new production processes (for example, using robots to assemble motor vehicles), invention also includes developments which do not incorporate any scientific advance (for example, the invention of the credit card or the introduction of the interest-bearing current account).

Innovation
Innovation is the commercial exploitation of the invention. Innovation includes the whole process whereby new technologies and products are brought to commercial fruition. Thus an invention may be a scientific discovery; innovation its economic application. Clearly, innovation will not occur unless the entrepreneur considers that it is worth while to commercialize the invention.

Schumpeter argued that the entrepreneur is not usually an inventor or explorer, because inventions or discoveries by themselves have little economic effect. For inventions or resource discoveries to be significant someone with the special talent for seeing their economic potential and bringing them into use must come along: that means the entrepreneur. Indeed, for Schumpeter, 'Innovation is possible without anything we should identify as invention.'

Schumpeter identified five major forms of innovation:

- the introduction of a new product or service, or an improvement in the quality of an existing good
- the introduction of a new method of production – this may be founded on a new scientific discovery but may also occur by finding new applications for existing scientific knowledge
- the development of a new market
- the exploitation of a new source of supply of raw materials or semi-manufactured goods
- the reorganization of the operation of an industry – for example, the creation of a monopoly position or the breaking up of a monopoly position.

For Schumpeter the entrepreneur is the person who sees the opportunity for innovation in any of the forms outlined above. The entrepreneur raises the finance to initiate innovation, assembles the factors of production, selects top managers and sets the organization going.

A distinguishing feature of Schumpeter's view is that he stresses that the entrepreneur need not be a 'capitalist', in that the entrepreneur does not necessarily have to use his own funds for business purposes. He also excluded risk from his view of the entrepreneur, arguing that risk-bearing is the function of the capitalist who lends his funds to the entrepreneur. For Schumpeter the entrepreneur bears risk only in so far as he invests his own funds in business activity:

'Risk obviously always falls on the owner of the means of production or of the money-capital which was paid for them, hence never on the entrepreneur *as such*.'

It should be noted that Schumpeter's concept of innovation is much wider than that currently used. Innovation for Schumpeter covers the doing of any new thing, or old thing in a new way. In this he differs from the current usage of the term in two main ways:

1. Schumpeter's definition covers anything that has not been done before, including for example two firms merging; whereas current usage restricts innovation to those events connected with the

appearance of new processes or products that have at least some technological content.

2. His rigid distinction between invention and innovation is regarded as unhelpful, in that it diverts attention away from the interdependence normally present between the various stages of the innovation process.

The modern concept of innovation is that it is a *process*, one of the early stages of which is invention. For the innovation process to continue beyond the stage of invention, action must be taken to apply the invention in a way which results in its successful utilization. This usually involves development, followed in turn by investment in productive capacity and by commercial launching.

Diffusion
Diffusion is the spread of an innovation through the industry and economy. A firm which successfully innovates will prompt rivals who are concerned about their competitive positions to attempt the innovation also. It is necessary, therefore, to distinguish between innovation and imitation. Only the first firm to introduce a new product or process change is usually regarded as the innovator; firms which subsequently adopt the innovation are referred to as imitators. As a result of widespread imitations, the innovation will become well established and may eventually form the basis for future inventions and subsequent innovation.

The entrepreneur and economic development
Schumpeter placed great stress on the leading role of the entrepreneur in **economic development** under capitalism. He starts his analysis with a model of the economy where all markets are in equilibrium. Innovation from whatever source will, however, cause disequilibrium because it will change the existing pattern of production.

The disturbance to equilibrium, therefore, comes in the form of an innovation. The innovation entails the construction of new plant and equipment and may do so in any of three different ways:

1. It may quicken the replacement of existing plant and equipment by making it obsolete.
2. It may create an expectation of high profit for the first firm in the new field, so encouraging an increase in total investment.
3. It may produce a new product that seems so attractive that people are willing to reduce their savings to purchase it. Since savings fall,

total expenditure rises and the implied increase in demand may lead to an increase in investment.

Schumpeter stressed the second of these types of expansionary process. He also assumed that the construction of new plant and equipment would be undertaken by new firms. This is precisely what happened in the case of railways, steam ships, automobiles, chemicals and other major innovations of the past two hundred years.

Once the innovator has demonstrated the profitability of his new venture, other firms will enter the market. Schumpeter argues that the first innovations will be made by the most talented entrepreneurs. Once those prove successful other less talented entrepreneurs will be encouraged to follow suit. In effect, there is a 'swarm' of imitators. A wave of innovation then follows which leads to the development of a new industry. The introduction of railways, for example, led to the construction of new towns, relocation of old industries, expansion of the iron and steel industry, etc. The development of the car industry brought with it the move to the suburbs, the construction of major roads, the development of new recreation centres, enormous expansion of the petroleum industry and rubber industries, etc. A significant innovation, such as railways or automobiles, can thus generate a huge wave of new investment through its direct and indirect effects on the economy, thus leading to growth and development.

The distinctive feature of Schumpeter's theory is the emphasis on entrepreneurship as the vital force in the whole economy. Schumpeter is very explicit about the economic function of the entrepreneur: he is the prime mover in economic development and his function is to innovate whether a new product, a new process, or internal reorganization.

Conclusions

As Professor M. Casson put it:

> 'Schumpeter, perhaps more than any other writer, is very explicit about the economic function of the entrepreneur. The entrepreneur is the prime mover in economic development and his function is to innovate or to "carry out new combinations".'

Schumpeter's view of the entrepreneur is clearly at odds with that of the tradition of Knight where it is maintained that the key role of the entrepreneur lies in risk-taking. Schumpeter, in contrast, argued that it is the capitalist who bears the risk.

With respect to the factors affecting innovation, economists have differing views over the influence of market structure and firm size on innovation. It is probable, however, that those firms which most actively pursue innovation are large firms with a high degree of market power and are more likely to be found in industries or sectors where scientific and technical advances are most rapid.

KEY WORDS

Invention	Process innovation
Innovation	Organizational innovation
Diffusion	Latent demand
Economic development	Research and development
Product innovation	Market power

Essay topics
1. How will product innovation affect the demand curve for the innovating firm's product?
2. 'The entrepreneur is the prime mover in economic development.' Explain this view.
3. Distinguish between an entrepreneur and a capitalist. In your view, who is the risk-bearer?
4. Distinguish clearly between 'invention' and 'innovation' and give examples of each. Are innovations possible without new scientific inventions?
5. Is innovation more likely to occur under conditions of perfect competition or monopoly?

Reading list
Drucker, P.F., *Innovation and Entrepreneurship: Practice and Principles*, Heinemann, 1985.

Harbury, C., *Workbook in Introductory Economics*, 4th edition, Pergamon 1988.

PROFILE: Anita Roddick, founder of Body Shop

Anita Roddick was astonished by the ease of her success – which was due, she says, to breaking nearly all the rules. The following insight, by Norma Wright, appeared in the magazine British Business *on 11 December 1987.*

* * *

The Body Shop International, named 'Company of the Year' at the 1987 Business Enterprise Awards, has a current annual turnover of more than £17.5m and almost 300 branches in 31 countries around the world. It has created almost 3000 new jobs – and 98 per cent of its products are made in Britain. The inspiration for it all has been its livewire founder and managing director.

'Unemployable' is how Anita Roddick describes herself – but as head of the largest British-owned retail chain overseas, she needn't worry. A former student teacher and United Nations employee in Geneva, she is now the supreme entrepreneur – with a highly unorthodox view of what that means.

'I believe people are confusing entrepreneurship with opportunism,' she said in a recent lecture at the City University Business School. 'They measure success by the profit and loss sheet.

'In reality, entrepreneurship consists of three things: first, the idea one wants to get across; second, oneself – the person promoting it; third, the money that's necessary to make it happen. The third is the least important of all; the first is what matters – the integrity of the idea. You just have to believe in what you're doing so strongly that it becomes a reality.

'Logically anybody who starts a small business with no money (as I did) can't succeed. But sometimes you do. Because you know if you don't succeed, you don't eat.'

Succeed she certainly did – and in an industry once described by Elizabeth Arden as 'the nastiest business in the world'.

Anita Roddick started her first shop in Brighton 11 years ago, with a loan of £4000 and some revolutionary ideas. She wanted to sell simple herbal and plant-based cosmetics, many of which she had seen used to great effect during her travels abroad; she intended to use the minimum amount of packaging and advertising; and she was determined to sell products that were developed with concern for the environment and were not tested on animals.

Inevitably the business had some teething troubles. The very first Body Shop had as neighbours a couple of funeral parlours who, not unnaturally, objected to its name; and her initial products 'looked and smelled peculiar' because the natural ingredients hadn't been prettified in any way. 'We had to explain to customers why our products looked revolting,' said Anita Roddick. And she only had 15 products in her range 'which looked pretty pathetic in the shop, because they only filled one shelf.'

She now has a range of over 300 products. The Body Shop still uses the cheapest bottles. 'The *Sunday Times* called them urine sample bottles, and perhaps they are' Mrs Roddick said. There are now five sizes of each product. 'Because we had so few products at first, we originated the idea of five sizes; then we could fill a whole wall of the shop.' Customers have taken to the idea of a wide range of sizes; they can try the small one first, before splashing out on the more expensive sizes.

Today's Body Shop is a franchise operation, each individual shop being 'almost a licence to print money' in Mrs Roddick's words. The franchising came about almost by accident.

'All our "unique" marketing features happened because we had no money. Because it cost £3000–£4000 to open up a shop about a decade ago, my husband Gordon and I dreamed up what we called the "self-financing" idea; we didn't even know the word "franchising". Now we have a network of marvellous franchisees.'

Community project undertaking

She selects her franchisees with extreme care. Not for her is the man who wants to set up his wife in a little business, because it would be fun and should make a bit of money. She looks for franchisees who share her aims and ideals – and insists that each should undertake some kind of community project.

'This is not only altruism – it's survival. We have community projects which are riveting. They range from running drug dependency groups and visiting elderly or handicapped people, to setting up street theatre. Most of our shops are run by women, who are enthusiastic about community work. And it's all done during working hours, not in their own time.'

Anita Roddick has an enormous fund of ideas – 'drawers full of them', she said.

And she's an expert communicator. The Body Shop publishes a bi-monthly 'Talksheet' for all members of staff, which contains – amongst others – a swop-a-job feature: staff are encouraged to exchange jobs for a few months, so a girl working in Bondi Beach can sample life in Aberdeen, and vice-versa.

Every month a video magazine, 'Talk Shop', is produced by the Body Shop's own video and film production company, and distributed to the franchisees worldwide. It includes reports on the various community projects and on Mrs Roddick's overseas trips: she travels for two months of every year, to find out how people in other cultures take care of their skin and hair, and to visit the various third world projects which produce products – for example, cosmetic sponges – for her shops.

There is also a series of leaflets published for individual customers and for schools, containing detailed product information; and newsletters posted up in the shops. Customers' opinions are actively sought. 'Can you imagine,' said Anita Roddick, 'that we are the only high street retailer which has suggestion boxes in its shops? Why spend billions of pounds on market research if you can do it yourself?'

She sees customer education as a major role. 'We reckon that about 25 million people must pass our shops at one time or another, so we use our windows to promote environmental community issues. Every one of our shops is like a major poster site.'

She is super-confident about the future, predicting 'we will become a major communications company and within two years we plan to have a magazine.' She also hopes to open a Body Shop in Moscow in three years' time.

'We think following the route of promoting health is vital for the cosmetics industry – it will not succeed by any other route. In the past it has often tried to create needs that don't really exist. We do things differently. It's so easy to break rules.'

Her advice to young potential entrepreneurs is simple: 'Never stop annoying people, and never stop asking questions. It is knowledge that gives you strength.'

Chapter Five

The entrepreneur and profit

'In all labour there is profit.'   Proverb

Profit is the reward to the entrepreneur. This chapter considers how profit is treated in standard economic theory and in each of the different views of the entrepreneur so far discussed. It is necessary first, however, to consider exactly what the economist means by 'profit'.

Profit: normal and abnormal

To the economist profit arises when a firm's total revenue exceeds its total cost (clearly if total cost exceeds total revenue the firm makes a loss). This concept of profit differs, though, from the accounting view of profit because the nature of costs differs between the two. The accounting concept of profit only takes into account explicit costs, while the economist takes into account both these and implicit costs.

Explicit and implicit costs

Explicit costs are direct charges on the business – such as the payment of wages and salaries, interest payments on borrowed funds, rates and rent and provision for the depreciation of capital stock. Some of these explicit costs will be fixed costs (they will not vary with output), such as rent and rates, fixed interest payments, depreciation and other overhead charges. Other explicit costs will be variable costs (the level of costs varies as output varies); for example, wage costs will rise if more labour is required to increase output, and similarly with raw material, fuel and energy costs.

Implicit costs arise when the entrepreneur also provides his or her own labour, capital and land to a business. The **opportunity cost** to the entrepreneur of doing so must be taken into account. Opportunity cost is a measure of the economic cost of using resources in one line of production in terms of the alternative forgone. Implicit wage, rent and interest costs must be taken into account, therefore, when the entrepreneur could have obtained wages by working for someone else, earned interest by investing his capital in someone else's business, and obtained rent by hiring his land to another person.

Normal and abnormal profit

Normal profit is the rate of profit which is just sufficient to ensure that a firm will continue to supply its existing good or service. The normal profit is the *opportunity cost* of the entrepreneur's services. Unless the entrepreneur obtains a reward equal to normal profit for undertaking activity in the present line of business he will leave one market and enter another where he believes the profit level earned will be at least the normal expected return.

These concepts are illustrated in Figure 2, which shows the usual U-shaped average total-cost curve labelled ATC; at a level of output of 100 units the ATC is £20.

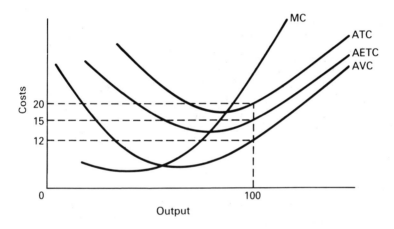

Figure 2 Cost curves used to demonstrate normal profit (see the text for an explanation)

The curve labelled AVC is the average variable-cost curve and shows those explicit costs which vary with output. The AVC is £12 at an output level of 100 units. The curve labelled AETC shows the average explicit total costs of production. The vertical distance between AETC and AVC thus measures the explicit fixed cost of production. The 'accounting costs' of production are thus shown by the AETC curve. At an output level of 100 units the average explicit total costs are £15, of which the average explicit fixed costs are £3.

The ATC curve is the economist's measure of the costs of production. The vertical distance between the ATC and AETC curves measures the implicit costs of production. This distance thus represents the opportunity costs to the entrepreneur (that is, it includes any implicit wages, rent and interest) and may be viewed as the measure of normal profit. At a level of output of 100 units with a price of £20, total revenue would equal total costs, but the entrepreneur would be earning a normal profit of £500 (i.e. 100 units × £5 difference between ATC and AETC). This rate of normal profit would be just enough to keep the entrepreneur operating in the same market.

Abnormal profit is the profit which is greater than that just sufficient to ensure that a firm will continue to supply its existing product. In other words, abnormal profit is the return over and above opportunity cost payments and hence is the profit earned over normal profit. Abnormal profit can therefore be defined as a residual which is left after all explicit and implicit costs have been met, including the transfer earnings or opportunity cost of the entrepreneur. There are a number of synonyms for abnormal profit, the common ones being super-normal profit, monopoly profit and pure profit.

Abnormal profits have an important role to play in the allocation of resources between markets. Abnormal profits will lead to an efficient allocation of resources if they encourage entrepreneurs to enter the market and increase supply. If, though, abnormal profits persist in the long run this indicates a distortion of the resource allocation process with monopoly suppliers being protected by barriers to entry. These factors are illustrated in the following sections.

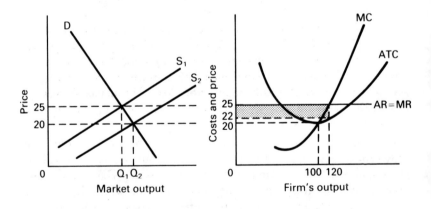

Figure 3 The market and firm under perfect competition

Perfectly competitive markets
Figure 3 shows the total market supply and demand curves of a **perfectly competitive market** and the revenue and cost curves of a typical firm operating in the market.

The initial position from the intersection of the demand curve and supply curve S_1 is that a market price of £25 is established. The individual firm, being a price taker, will seek to maximize profit by equating marginal revenue (= price) with marginal cost. The firm will therefore produce 120 units.

At an output level of 120 units the firm's ATC is £22. Hence the firm earns an abnormal profit of £360 in total (i.e. abnormal profit of £3 per unit × 120 units), shown by the shaded area in Figure 3. As firms in this market are earning profits in excess of normal profits this will attract new firms to the industry. Entrepreneurs will respond to the abnormal profit signal and transfer resources to the market in the hope of obtaining a return above the normal profit level. The influx of new firms to the market will lead to an increase in supply at each price level. Hence the market supply curve will shift to the right. This process will continue until the supply curve has shifted to S_2.

With supply curve S_2, given the market demand curve, the equilibrium price will now be £20. At a price of £20 the profit-maximizing output level (where the new MR = MC) will now be 100 units. At this level of output the firm's ATC is equal to the firm's AR (i.e. £20). Hence the abnormal profits have been eroded and each firm will be earning only normal profit. With only a normal profit level available in the market no new firms will seek to enter and the market will be in equilibrium.

The perfectly competitive market thus leads to the **optimum allocation** of scare resources with the supply of goods reflecting the pattern of consumer demand. The price of the product is equal to the minimum average total cost, including a normal profit return to entrepreneurs, which results in an optimal level of consumer welfare. This comes about because new firms are free to enter the market; there are no **barriers to entry**.

Monopoly markets

In contrast, where a market is characterized by **monopoly**, the output level will not respond to the signal of abnormal profits. Fewer resources will be devoted to producing the product than the pattern of consumer demand warrants.

Figure 4 depicts the profit-maximizing price–output combination for a monopolist. The monopolist equates marginal revenue with marginal cost to determine the profit-maximizing output level of Q_m. The quantity Q_m can be sold at a price of P_m, determined by the firm's demand curve. The average cost of producing Q_m, is, though, less than the average revenue, and the monopolist earns abnormal profit shown by the shaded area in Figure 4. Although the monopolist is earning abnormal profit and firms will wish to enter the market, they will be prevented from doing so by entry barriers – the following chapter considers the nature of barriers to entry.

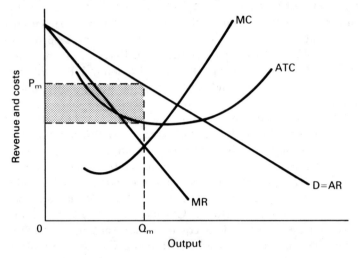

Figure 4 The profit-maximizing equilibrium of a monopolist

Under monopoly, therefore, there will be a smaller quantity supplied to the market and the price will be higher than under perfect competition. Where barriers to entry prevent entrepreneurs from responding to the signal of abnormal profit, prices will exceed the real resource costs of supplying the product (i.e. price exceeds marginal cost) and the market mechanism will not lead to the optimum allocation of resources. It is because of this outcome that governments adopt a policy of preventing the growth of private-sector monopolies – for example through the Monopolies and Mergers Commission prohibiting one large firm taking over another in order to obtain a dominant position in the market.

Profits and marginal productivity theory of income distribution

In standard economic theory the entrepreneur is viewed as one of the factors of production along with labour, capital and land. According to the marginal productivity theory of income distribution, factor inputs will be paid rewards equal to the value of their **marginal revenue products.** Under conditions of perfect competition, for example, the marginal revenue product is given by the marginal physical product (the quantity of output produced by an extra unit of variable factor input) multiplied by the price of the product. There are problems, however, in attempting to apply the marginal productivity theory of factor earnings to the entrepreneur.

Firstly, it is not possible to measure the marginal revenue product of the entrepreneur to an individual firm. Entrepreneurship is not divisible, it is a fixed unit. The marginal product of entrepreneurship to the firm, therefore, can only be the difference between the total output of the firm *with* the entrepreneur and the total output *without* the entrepreneur. In the latter case output would be zero, since in fact there would not be a firm. Hence it would have to be argued that the marginal product of entrepreneurship is the total output of the firm and thus the reward to the entrepreneur should be the whole of the firm's revenue, which is clearly untenable.

Secondly, for marginal productivity theory to apply, factor inputs are assumed to be homogeneous. In reality, however, entrepreneurs are too heterogeneous to permit discussion of 'standard units' of entrepreneurial inputs. Even if a standard entrepreneurial man-hour could be defined, it is unlikely that there would be any close relationship between the *quantity* supplied and the amount of service rendered in terms of the *quality* of supply. An hour's input from, say, Robert Maxwell is likely to be significantly different from that of most entrepreneurs running a small firm.

It is not possible, therefore, to treat the reward of the entrepreneur in the standard manner as is the case for the other factor inputs according to marginal productivity theory. Alternative theories of profit are briefly considered in the following sections.

The uncertainty theory of profit

Following on from Knight's theory of the entrepreneur (considered in Chapter 3), profit arises as a result of the constantly changing environment in which the firm operates and the associated uncertainty concerning the outcomes of alternative courses of action. Profit is the residual (if any) left for the entrepreneur after he has paid the contractual payments agreed for the factor inputs he hires. The entrepreneur is identified as being ultimately in control of the venture and thus ultimately responsible for all costs and all revenues. The entrepreneur is thus subject to the uncertainty which surrounds the amount and sign of the difference between total costs and total revenue.

Uncertainty in the economic environment means that the *anticipated* value of goods or services produced may differ from the *actual* value realized, with profit the compensation to the entrepreneur for shouldering this uncertainty.

Adherants of this theory argue that the profit-maximizing assumption in the standard theory of the firm has nothing to do with pure profits which are generated within the dynamic context, by uncertainty and change. This is because pure profit cannot be deliberately maximized in advance of productive activity, but is the outcome of productive activity. Profits cannot be positive unless there is a non-insurable uncertainty. The role of the entrepreneur is to shoulder the burden of uncertainty and therefore take the reward of profit.

The innovation theory of profit

According to Schumpeter, entrepreneurship consists in introducing new processes of production – of producing new products or producing old products in new ways (see Chapter 4). The entrepreneur disturbs the economic flow of production and the market equilibrium where abnormal profits are zero by creating new ways of doing things and new things to do. In fulfilling this role he is at the same time creating profits for himself. By breaking away from established, routine activity, the entrepreneur is able to generate temporary gaps between the prices of inputs and the price of output. The innovating entrepreneur is thus able to reap abnormal profits until imitators once again force prices and costs into equilibrium and hence abnormal profit returns to zero.

The arbitrage theory of profit

According to this view profit opportunities arise where the prices of goods are high compared with the costs of factor inputs. In effect, 'something' is being sold at different prices in the two markets as a result of imperfect communication between the markets. Economically the bundle of inputs in the factor market and the consumption goods in the product market are the same thing. If though the entrepreneur notices that the total cost of the factor inputs is less than the total revenue expected for the sale of the good then an opportunity arises for making profits.

At the time of the decision to produce a product its price may not yet exist, although it is anticipated by the entrepreneur. The entrepreneur believes that future product prices are not fully reflected in today's input prices. Profits arise from an absence of adjustment between the goods market and the factor market and successful entrepreneurship consists in noticing such maladjustments before others do.

Do entrepreneurs seek to maximize profits?

The usual assumption in economics is that the firm attempts to establish that price–output combination which maximizes profit. The goal of profit maximization is attained where marginal cost equals marginal revenue. The notion that firms attempt to maximize profit has however come under considerable attack. Firstly, it is argued that firms do not have the necessary knowledge, information or ability to equate MC and MR. Secondly, it is argued that firms may have goals other than profit maximization.

Imperfect information and uncertainty

Firms operate in conditions of imperfect information and uncertainty; therefore entrepreneurs do not have the necessary information which enables them to equate marginal cost and marginal revenue. In practice the demand curve of the firm is not known with certainty. The entrepreneur will not be entirely aware of consumers' preferences and will be unsure of competitors' reactions and how they will affect the demand for their product. If the demand schedule is not known then the marginal revenue schedule will also not be known by the entrepreneur. Also, the marginal cost curve may not be known. Conventional accounting practices do not readily allow the entrepreneur to identify marginal cost while in multiproduct firms (i.e. in firms producing more than one product), the identification of marginal cost for a particular product line may be extremely difficult. Moreover, because of uncertainty in the economic environment, entrepreneurs will lack accurate knowledge of future demand and cost conditions. Critics conclude, therefore, that because the demand and cost curves of the firm cannot be objectively known the profit maximizing objective is unattainable.

Alternative goals

Dissatisfaction with profit maximization as the sole basis for motivating business behaviour has led observers to propose a number of alternative goals. The alternatives are believed to provide a more realistic underpinning for explaining and predicting the behaviour of the firm.

Satisficing behaviour

Given the uncertainty in the real world and the lack of accurate information some writers have suggested that the firm will not be able to act to maximize any objective. Instead firms behave in a *satisficing* manner: they pursue 'satisfactory profits', 'satisfactory growth', etc. This behaviour is considered rational given the uncertainty of the real world.

Revenue maximization

A frequently mentioned alternative to profit maximization is that of revenue maximization. It is contended that once profits reach acceptable levels firms are inclined to place higher sales revenue ahead of higher profits as the main objective. Firms do this because sales revenue is a key indicator of business performance, tending to reflect consumer acceptance of a firm's product, its competitive position in the market place and growth.

Market share goals

Some writers argue that many firms set as their goal the attainment and retention of a constant market share. A large market share can be a valuable asset because it reflects a firm's ability to compete effectively and to benefit from scale economies and being a recognized market leader.

Long-run survival goals

Some writers have suggested that the primary motive of the entrepreneur is long-run survival. Entrepreneurs will therefore take action which maximizes the probability that they will survive over the indefinite future. In this regard, higher sales, profits and market share are relevant because they contribute to the long-run survival and viability of the firm.

These and other goals have been suggested as alternatives to the profit maximizing objective. The empirical evidence regarding the goals of firms is inconclusive. What most studies do indicate though is that most businesses have a multiplicity of goals and that those running the firm do not have unlimited discretion in setting their goals. It appears, however, that there is a minimum profit level which firms must at least make in order to pursue other goals.

Conclusions

Profit plays an important role in economic theory in terms of acting as a signal to entrepreneurs to transfer resources to where they can best fulfil consumer demands. This process only operates effectively if there are no entry barriers to markets where abnormal profit is being earned.

Profit differs from other factor rewards in a number of ways. It cannot be related to some quantity of entrepreneurial activity, because there are no units of measurement, such as an hour's work in which it can be measured. Profit is not contractual but residual: it is uncertain and fluctuates more widely than other incomes. Hence the entrepreneur never knows in advance what profits will be and does not even know for certain if there will be any profits.

Associated with each theory of the entrepreneur is a theory of profit; whether entrepreneurs attempt to maximize profits is an open question. It is clear, though, that a firm must attain a minimum acceptable level of profit in order to remain in business.

KEY WORDS

Explicit costs
Implicit costs
Opportunity cost
Normal and abnormal
   profit
Perfectly competitive
   market

Optimum allocation
Barriers to entry
Monopoly
Marginal revenue
   products

Essay topics

1. A manager in a large company resigned his salaried £18 000 job and started his own business. He invested £20 000 of his own savings, which had been in a building society account earning 10 per cent annual interest, to purchase land, premises and capital equipment for the business. At the end of the first year of trading he calculated that his total costs were £30 000 while his total revenue was £50 000, and announced himself pleased with a first year's profit of £20 000. What level of profit would an economist say that he had made?
2. What role do profits play in the allocation of resources?
3. 'Profits are the reward for bearing the burden of uncertainty'. Discuss this statement and identify those who earn the reward in modern business organizations.
4. Outline and evaluate a theory of profit.

Reading list

Anderton, A.G., Chapter 28 in *Economics: A New Approach*, UTP, 1984.

Begg, D., Fischer, S. and Dornbusch, R., Chapter 6 in *Economics*, 2nd edn, McGraw-Hill, 1987.

Harbury, C., *Workbook in Introductory Economics*, 4th edition, Pergamon, 1988, p. 49.

Hrywniak, M. and Smith, P., 'Beware of false-profits', *Economic Review*, Jan. 1989.

Lipsey, R.G., *Positive Economics*, 6th edn, Weidenfeld & Nicolson, 1983, pp. 318–20, 327–28.

Maunders, P., Myers, D. and Wall, N., *Economics Explained*, Collins Educational, 1988, pp. 313–15.

PROFILE: Alan Sugar, founder of Amstrad plc

Alan Sugar is not known for currying favour with the City. Why should he? He has pushed Amstrad from nowhere into the billion pound league. The following assessment, by Bernard Gray, appeared in Investors Chronicle *on 1 July 1988.*

* * *

Alan Sugar does not suffer fools at all. He runs Amstrad efficiently and expects others to meet his exacting standards, particularly his critics in the City. 'I hate inefficiency. I hate it in my own company and I hate it in those analysts who know as much about the electronics sector as I know about knitting a pullover.' Jibes like that go some way towards explaining both the success of Amstrad in recent years and the poor state of relations between Sugar and City analysts.

The success has been hard-won. When Sugar started Amstrad 20 years ago the first venture was manufacturing and selling turntable covers. He expanded into the full range of hi-fi, sourcing many of his products in the Far East and operating a tightly-knit marketing group in Britain.

This was to become the pattern for future operations; Sugar drove hard deals with Oriental suppliers and UK retailers. Keen pricing and flexibility of supply are key elements in the company's strategy and the structure enables Sugar to switch from one product to another very quickly, following or indeed anticipating, changes in consumer tastes.

Amstrad grew steadily and the company was floated on the stockmarket in 1980, but the real breakthrough for Sugar came with the move into personal computers in 1984. Turnover soared as he introduced affordable word processors and IBM compatible personal computers. Pre-tax profits grew from £9m in 1984 to £137m in 1987.

But many in the City remained sceptical of Amstrad's success. They felt that for momentum to be maintained, Sugar must produce a continuing stream of big-selling new products and additionally viewed the company as a one man band.

As yet Amstrad has confounded the doubters, and blossomed into one of the FT-SE 100 companies, valued at over £1bn. Sugar still retains a large part of the equity, making his personal fortune over £500m on paper. Does he keep such a substantial stake in the company in order to give him greater control or to make the firm bid-proof? 'No', says Sugar defensively: 'I would be criticised if I owned 50 per cent of the company or none.'

His huge personal share stake must at the least reinforce him as the dominant presence at Amstrad. However, he emphasises that decisions are not made solely by him, but by a small team of senior managers collectively. Until recently that group shared an open plan room where they could shout information to each other. His new office may be a more conventional environment for a chief executive, but Sugar says he misses the hurly-burly.

In any event the company remains a close-knit unit. Amstrad employs only 1000 people and Sugar feels they all share his enthusiasm for efficiency. 'The cliche that people stay at Amstrad for two minutes or a lifetime is probably true,' he confesses. And the commitment to efficiency seems to be genuine: headquarters is a modest block in Brentwood, not a flashy West End address.

Sugar believes that the company must remain small and avoid bureaucracy if it is not to become 'like all the rest of those companies'. He thinks he can do this and maintain growth by selling bigger ticket items. 'You put the same energy and emotion into selling something for £5 or £500. Why not sell one at £500 and get on with the next sale?' Yet despite his efforts to keep the operation manageable, it has necessarily grown from the early days.Two areas where Sugar accepts that his working methods have had to change are research and development, where seat of the pants skills are no longer enough, and foreign exchange exposure, now controlled by a treasury department. He has had to devolve some power to other senior managers and says he spends part of his time doing deals and part managing people. But perhaps his most crucial contribution remains an unparalleled feel for markets, acknowledged by others in the field like Sir Clive Sinclair.

Although naturally decisive, Sugar can be cautious in business. Amstrad's success has come from exploiting gaps in existing markets, not in developing new fields. This makes his recent decision to enter the emerging satellite TV business seem a little out of character, but Sugar is confident. 'There is nothing new about TV, all we are offering is a new way to receive programmes. In that sense it is not a new market at all.' A recent survey showed little public appetite for satellite TV – but Sugar's 'feel' could be vindicated yet again.

In Amstrad's mainstream business of making and marketing personal computers, Sugar thinks that existing products offer good prospects for continuing growth.

'If we can achieve the same sort of market share in Germany or Italy as we have in France or Britain then we will have enough growth to last at least five years, even without any new products.' He also reckons that 1992 will bring opportunities for Amstrad by forcing common technical standards rather than opening up closed markets. 'We were picked by the Government for some advertisements in the 1992 campaign because we are an example of a company that is already getting it right on the Continent.'

He is a lot more cautious about the American market, and refuses to buy market share in the US by cutting margins. 'We are in business to make money. That may seem remarkable to some people.'

Confident of his strategy, Sugar is not at all afraid of the competition either from America or from Japan. 'The Japanese will not dominate computers the way they dominate hi-fi. They are just programmed ants. They have no flair. All of the originality comes from Britain or America but they are no good at manufacturing.' (You can feel his PR advisers wince.)

Alan Sugar sounds like a pattern Thatcherite businessman. But he shows as little respect for Mrs T's entrepreneurial renaissance as he does for City wheeling and dealing. 'Some things lend themselves to manufacture in Britain, but I haven't noticed any difference in the last ten years.' Hostile takeovers? 'I am a great believer in organic growth. I don't think that contested takeovers bring half the benefits claimed. All our acquisitions have been careful and logical.'

His aggressive attitude to the City, though not helpful to the share price, is easy to understand. Sugar is one of Britain's most successful businessmen and has scant respect for critics who seem to have few qualifications for the job, save those gained in a university. He may be less articulate than the slickers, but has built a real business.

Despite this dislike for the City and its background of privilege, even Sugar does not totally ignore the moneymen. A tele-text TV in his office constantly displays the latest stockmarket news.

Money may no longer be the prime motivation for Sugar, but some things are universal. On his office wall there is a framed cheque for £25m from the company, made out to the Inland Revenue – clearly paying tax is painful at Amstrad too.

Chapter Six

The entrepreneur and new firm formation

'Nearly 200 000 new businesses a year are being set up and this upsurge in the spirit of enterprise must be encouraged and supported.' Mrs Margaret Thatcher

The purpose of this chapter is to consider the factors influencing new firm formation. The establishment (and subsequent success or failure) of a new enterprise represents the culmination of a series of complex processes. It should be stressed that a new enterprise is neither the product of simple market forces nor the personal desire to be 'one's own boss'. Rather, it is a combination of a huge range of personal (sociological and psychological), situational (geographic) and related factors (making up the economic and work environment).

It is also generally argued that there is no single 'moment of creation' of a new firm but rather three major phases:

1. *Incubation* of the project by the founder. This aspect will be discussed in more detail later in the chapter.
2. *Preparation*, when major options are taken and start-up resources are gathered.
3. *Start-up* of the new enterprise.

To some observers this sequence indicates that the process of new firm formation starts by being essentially psycho-sociological and becomes progressively more economic in nature and concerned with management of resources as the new business takes form.

Expected profit and barriers to entry

It is generally assumed that an increase in the rate of profit earned in a particular industry will cause firms to enter that industry. Clearly not all firms entering the industry will be new ones established for the first time to take advantage of the profit opportunities, as some entrants will be existing firms transferring from one industry to another. Despite this the rate of new firm formation in an industry will be linked to the prospective profit opportunities available there. This view is based on the conventional argument that the entrepreneur is in the risk business – he takes risks in the expectation of profit. It follows that the flow of prospective entrepreneurs into a particular industry will be linked to the existence of risky but potentially profitable gains.

It is also necessary to recognize, however, that entry into some industries is substantially more difficult than in others owing to the existence of barriers to entry: the heights of entry barriers will deter some potential entrants. Entry barriers may occur for a number of reasons.

The absolute cost advantage of existing firms

Existing firms may be able to produce at lower cost than could any new and probably small competitor. Such an advantage may come from knowledge obtained by 'learning by doing' in the industry, or because established firms control key resources or hold patents (legal monopolies).

Scale economies of established firms

Established firms in an industry may have achieved **economies of scale** which puts them at an advantage compared with new entrants.

Figure 5 shows a new entrant with only a small share of the market producing Q_n units and with long-run average costs of C_n. This compares with an established firm with a large market share producing Q_e. The established firm has been able to exploit scale economies and has long-run average costs of C_e. Clearly the new firm will find it difficult to compete with the established firm.

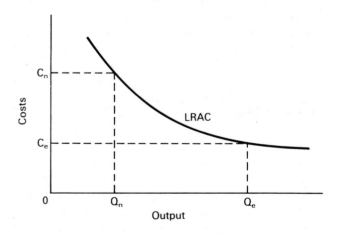

Figure 5 Long-run average costs for new and established firms

The absolute costs of starting a business

When the financial capital required to start a business is considerable this will act as a significant barrier to the entry of new firms to the industry. It may be expected, therefore, that the less it costs to set up in a particular industry the greater will be the number of enterprises that set up there.

It is also probable that the lower the cost of entry the fewer the number of sources of finance the entrepreneur would require. This would then lead to a greater dependence on personal finance and allow the entrepreneur a greater freedom of action than may be possible if institutional sources of finance were required. For example, a bank may limit the activity of an entrepreneur to particular ventures as a condition of extending a loan.

This argument may be taken further to distinguish between the rates of entry into manufacturing and the personal services sector. A large part of manufacturing has become so capital-intensive that this has restricted the entry of new small-scale businesses. Consequently, although some opportunities remain in manufacturing, the real possibilities for entrepreneurship are within the personal services sector, as it is within this sector that less initial capital is required. Compare, for example, the capital equipment required by a hairdresser or a window cleaner with that required in the production of hair-driers or ladders.

Product differentiation

Where established firms have distinctive brands or have used other marketing techniques to obtain a high degree of customer loyalty, new firms may have great difficulty in winning consumers away from established competitors. Hence, the more homogenous the product the easier it will be for new firms to enter the industry. An existing firm's heavily advertised '**brand image**' good is a barrier to entry both financially and psychologically.

Growth of the industry

The more rapid the growth rate in a particular industry the more likely it is to attract new firms, while a contracting industry is less likely to attract entrants.

This view is linked to the previous point that industries with higher rates of profit will cause firms to enter, in that an increase in growth rate may be regarded by a potential entrepreneur as an indication that there is a satisfactory level of profit to be made in that particular industry.

The proportion of total employment in the industry in small firms

Several commentators have suggested that the sizes of existing enterprises in an industry are a major factor determining new firm formation rates. This factor is associated with what is termed the **incubator hypothesis**. The man who works in a small firm is considered to be trained for entrepreneurship, since it is more likely that he will have to be involved with all aspects of the production process. The manager of a small firm, for example, has to be conversant with all aspects of managing the business; on the other hand, managers in large firms who have specialized in certain areas (production, accountancy, marketing, etc.) have tended to lose the all-round experience of managing a firm.

Also in the small firm, each employee is required to undertake a greater variety of tasks than workers in a larger firm. He will be encouraged to adopt a flexible approach to work; and, provided he does not appear to threaten the power position of the owner/manager, any initiatives on his part are likely to be rewarded. Experience of all aspects of running a business are likely to be available to him, and the individual may judge that he is able to run a business as well for himself as for somebody else.

Industrial structure

The empirical evidence strongly tends to support the view that it is from small firms that new enterprises are generated. However, while experience of working in a firm of a particular size may be an important factor, also of significance is the **industrial structure**.

The basic point here is that the entry of new firms into particular industries may well be related to the existing pattern of firm size in that industry. The presence of a large number of small firms may be a good indication that barriers to entry are low and/or that the optimum size of unit is small. It may be concluded, therefore, that the pattern of new firm births must be expected to follow the industrial pattern of small firms throughout British Industry.

The unemployment rate and other influences

Unemployment for an individual could provide the trigger mechanism which pushes him or her into entrepreneurship. For instance, on being made redundant a worker may wish to trust his future to himself rather than to others and seek to avoid a repetition of the disappointment redundancy may have brought. Further, the lump-sum payment which redundancy often brings provides the potential entrepreneur with the motive and at least part of the start-up finance required.

The personal characteristics of individuals are important in determining the emergence of new firm founders. It is apparent that individuals display vastly different degrees of entrepreneurial alertness. The qualities called for in successful entrepreneurship are thus not uniformly distributed across the population and certainly do not appear to be in infinite supply. A discussion of the social and psychological characteristics of entrepreneurs is not possible here, but it should be noted that an individual's personal characteristics and social background will greatly influence his or her willingness to become an entrepreneur.

The emergence and subsequent growth of new firms depends also on the general environmental conditions. These conditions are determined by such factors as political changes, the degree of state involvement in industry and the attitudes of the financial institutions. The ethos of the society in terms of the influences and attitudes towards entrepreneurship is important. This ethos will partly determine the degree of acceptability of new firm formation.

Closely associated with this is the general view towards risk-taking and society's attitude towards failure. One view is that while it is acceptable to be seen to try and fail in the USA, the negative attitude towards failure and bankruptcy in the UK is often a significant deterrent to risk-taking. Clearly such attitudes and influences are extremely difficult to measure, but at the margin are likely to have an important effect on the willingness of the pool of potential entrepreneurs actually to take the step to establish a business. Since 1979 the Conservative government has attempted to shift the prevailing attitude in Britain towards a more favourable view of entrepreneurship.

Conclusions

This chapter has identified some of the major factors influencing the state of new firm formation, both in particular industries and in the economy in general. These factors are numerous, but in terms of economic theory the most important influences are considered to be the industry's rate of profit, industry growth rate, the proportion of small firms in the industry and the rate of unemployment in the industry. Cutting across all of these factors, however, is the influence of industrial structure. Also of importance are the barriers to entry of the industry concerned. Other factors of note are the underlying cultural attitudes towards entrepreneurship and the personal characteristics of potential entrepreneurs.

```
┌─────────────────────────────────────────────────────────┐
│                      KEY WORDS                          │
│                                                          │
│   Expected profit          Incubator hypothesis         │
│   Barriers to entry        Industrial structure         │
│   Economies of scale       Unemployment                 │
│   Brand image                                           │
│                                                          │
└─────────────────────────────────────────────────────────┘
```

Essay topics

1. What are 'barriers to entry' and why may they deter new firm formation?
2. Explain the incubator hypothesis.
3. How may an industry's growth rate, level of profits and rate of unemployment affect the number of new firms established in the industry?
4. What influence does industrial structure have on new firm formation?

Data Response Question 3

Being your own boss

Read the accompanying article from the *Guardian* of 31 October 1988 and answer the following questions.

1. What do you understand by 'socially marginal people' and why would they be expected to become entrepreneurs?
2. Why might small-scale enterprise be thought to 'offer opportunities for the upwardly mobile'?
3. Distinguish between a 'small business owner' and 'the self-employed'. Why should these two groupings be treated as distinct types of economic activity?
4. In what sense is the small business sector a heterogeneous group?
5. 'Men outnumber women by three to one among small business owners, although among the self-employed the proportion of women is slightly higher.' How do you account for this?
6. What in your view is the prime motivator for becoming an entrepreneur?

The mythology of being your own boss

Running a small business should carry a health warning: small firms are started by socially marginal people on their way up; Asians are natural entrepreneurs and inevitably drawn to starting small businesses.

Everybody knows that this is the received wisdom, perceptions built up over the years, so it must be true. But is it?

These myths and legends about the small business community are strongly challenged in a fascinating and painstaking new study of small business owners and the self-employed.

It comes to the conclusion that working for yourself may be less stressful than working for other people.

And while Asians are more likely to start small businesses than Afro-Caribbeans, they are no more drawn to small firms than other minorities, especially Cypriots; in any case the overwhelming majority of Asians, more than 85 per cent, are employees.

While small-scale enterprise has often been thought to offer opportunities for the upwardly mobile, the children of employers, managers and other professionals are more than proportionately represented.

'In fact, small-scale enterprise could be more a catch-net for those downwardly mobile from more privileged social origins than an opportunity ladder for lower-strata members.'

These findings come from analysis of a previously neglected data source, the General Household Survey, by Mr James Curran, Midland Bank professor of small business studies at Kingston Polytechnic, and Mr Roger Burrows of North East London Polytechnic. The study covers the survey for the years 1979–84.

Almost one household in every five contacted by the government's Office of Population, Censuses and Surveys contained either a small business owner (employing fewer than 25 people) or someone self-employed, making it a rich and representative source of information about the country's fastest-growing economic sector.

The authors were able to analyse the responses of 5700 small business owners and self-employed, the latter group almost entirely ignored in the past both by government and researchers.

The conclusion which emerges most strongly, and which is repeated in almost every section of the report, is that the two groupings should be treated as distinct types of economic activity.

(For many years this point has been made after every Budget by the National Federation of Self-Employed and Small Businesses, the largest of the lobby groups in the field).

Self-employment should not be seen simply as a stage on the way to taking on employees.

In terms of the kind of economic activities in which the two populations engage, their age, gender profiles, and educational backgrounds, there are large differences.

Another factor which stands out from the analysis of such a broad representative sample is the heterogeneity of small business owners' economic involvement – highlighting the dangers of generalising about a small business 'sector'.

Small business research has tended to concentrate on manufacturing – the engineering firm with a handful of employees or the hi-tech firm making electronics equipment – but in fact only a little over 10 per cent of small firms are in manufacturing.

Among the self-employed the proportion in services and other non-manufacturing activities is even higher.

As might be expected, more than 90 per cent of women are in non-manufacturing, compared with just under 65 per cent of men.

The stresses of running a small business are often thought to take their toll on marriage, while, for women, small firm ownership or self-employment are seen as ways of achieving independence – but the survey supports neither of these notions.

Levels of marriage are similar to those in the rest of the working population, while divorce and separation are lower. The survey gives no indication of the quality of marital relations, of course, but does indicate that marriage and working for yourself can go together.

The data for 1979–84 shows the enormous growth of small-business owning and self-employed populations: in 1979 they represented just over 8 per cent of the employed population, but by 1984 had risen to more than 12 per cent.

Both men and women increased their numbers, but the relative proportions stayed broadly the same.

Men outnumber women by three to one among small business owners, although among the self-employed the proportion of women is slightly higher.

The study shows very clearly what has been called the 'age launch window' effect; the period in many people's lives when the combination of ambition, experience, energy and access to capital are at their most favourable for striking out.

Thus the most likely age is between 30 and 40, though those in self-employment are on average likely to be younger than small business owners.

The data also suggests a reluctance among both small types to retire, compared with the working population as a whole.

And is it all worth it in terms of material reward?

The study found that small business owners and the self-employed were making more money than they like to admit, but that they worked very hard for it.

On the basis of car and house ownership – seen as better indicators of wealth than published Inland Revenue data – small business owners and self-employed are better off than employees. The authors say that, while independence may be the prime motivator, 'this need not involve material sacrifices.'

The other side of the coin, however, is that more than half of male small firm owners worked more than 50 hours a week; while the self-employed worked less hard, three out of ten worked more than 50 hours a week.

One in five women small firm owners worked more than 50 hours a week, but more than half of self-employed women worked less than 20 hours.

Clive Woodcock

PROFILES: Managers turn entrepreneur

The following is based on an article which appeared in Management Today *in August 1986.*

* * *

A recent study of British managers by Professor Richard Scase and Dr Robert Goffee uncovered considerable enthusiasm for small business start-ups of all kinds. Their research showed that many dissatisfied managers are very keen to leave the shelters of corporate life and set up in business for themselves. They surveyed over 300 managers, aged 25–65, in a broad cross-section of industries. Of those interviewed, at least 59 per cent had seriously considered starting their own businesses. Age was an important factor: almost 70 per cent of the under-35s had considered a start-up, compared with less than half of those over 45. More than 20 per cent of those surveyed believed that their companies were not making the best use of their managerial talents, and of these two-thirds were thinking of setting up their own businesses.

Scase and Goffee found that the sort of manager who wants to start his own business has a strong need for self-fulfilment, creativity, and opportunities for independent judgement. It is because this need is not met in their managerial positions that such people want to start their own businesses. Other motivators include the fact that 'the cost of career pursuit greatly outweighs the benefits', 'employment inhibits personal growth', and 'small-scale organizations are more satisfying places to work than large ones'. These managers are not dissatisfied with the work itself: it is the organizational conditions which frustrate them. For most managers a business start-up represents an opportunity to pursue work more fully.

Blackman hits the screen

Ken Blackman, a former marketing executive with Intel, the silicon chip manufacturer, left to start up 01 Computers for a variety of reasons – including a desire for personal wealth, the wish not to work for anyone else and wanting to build something of his own 'rather than being a small cog in a large wheel'.

01 Computers was set up to supply microcomputer-based solutions to business users. There are three trading divisions: 01 Computers, supplying complete computer systems to business users, which won an IBM quality award in 1985; 01 Consultancy, offering comprehensive training courses for personal computer users in programming and microcomputer applications; and Paradigm, which identifies and markets high-quality, leading-edge computer products to extend the capabilities of PCs.

Blackman, 30, aims to achieve USM listing in 'as short a time as possible'. The group is growing fast – currently turnover is £5 million with profits of 10 per cent. The target is a turnover of £10 million, still with 10 per cent profits, by 1988, by when Blackman would like to be publicly quoted. By continuing this spanking growth rate, he hopes to gain the confidence of the City. Once he has that, 'I intend to use this to gear up to either a full listing, or to acquire further finance for other ventures'.

Chamberlain's new number

Peter Chamberlain became frustrated by the big-company bureaucracy after a career with Xerox, Mars and finally British Telecom, where he was a sales operations director. When he came under pressure from venture capital companies eager to take advantage of Telecom's liberalization, 42-year-old Chamberlain eventually decided to realize his long-held ambition to 'go it alone' (and make money).

He founded National Telephone Systems in 1978 with Robin Bailey, to develop and market a range of small-to-medium business telephone systems. The company sells through a range of dealers and distributors in the

UK and is expanding rapidly abroad. All manufacturing is sub-contracted in the UK through Thorn Ericsson. For the future, relationships are being formed with Far East countries for certain products and markets.

NTS now turns over £5–6 million, increasing to £7–8 million by year-end March 1987. If all goes to plan, turnover should be £21 million by 1988–89, with profits of £2.4 million. To do this, the company must 'continue the pace and development which has already made us the fastest-growing British telecoms company'. NTS aims to support the new emergent distribution channels in the UK and to secure a solid base in the home market while expanding internationally.

Chapter Seven
The small firm

'Today's new, small firms are the seed bed for tomorrow's merchant venturers.' Mrs Margaret Thatcher

For many observers this is the age of the entrepreneur. Following a long period of neglect those who start and manage their own businesses are now viewed with admiration. They are seen as risk-takers and innovators who are prepared to reject the relative security of employment to create wealth and accumulate capital on their own behalf. There has also been a new emphasis on the small-firm sector as a source of economic recovery. This contrasts sharply with the decades of the 1950s and 1960s when small entrepreneurial ventures were often regarded as unproductive and inefficient.

The neglect of small firms
From the end of the Second World War up to the early 1970s, much of government industrial policy was designed to encourage large-scale corporations in order to facilitate economic growth. It was generally agreed that the creation of large business units, which often came about through mergers, was necessary to reap the benefits of econo-mies of scale in order to enable UK firms to compete internationally. Such thinking led the government in 1966 to set up the Industrial Reorganization Corporation (IRC) to encourage the reorganization of UK industry. In practice this led the IRC to promote mergers through financial and other assistance. The IRC was dismantled in 1971, when the emphasis on increasing size as a means of achieving greater efficiency began to wane and there was a gradual renewal of interest in small firms.

What is a small firm?
Exactly what constitutes a 'small business' is open to debate and the search for a definition of a small firm goes back many years. The **Bolton Committee** in 1971 argued that a small firm has a number of characteristics:

- It has a relatively small market share.
- The firm is managed in a personalized way by its owner.
- It is independent and does not form part of a larger company.

Table 1 Statistical definitions of the small-firm sector

Business sector	Number of employees	Turnover (£000)	
		Bolton Committee* (1963 prices)	Revised to allow for inflation to 1983
Manufacturing	200		
Construction	25		
Mining/quarrying	25		
Retailing		50	315
Wholesale trades		200	1260
Motor trade		100	630
Miscellaneous services		50	315
Road transport	5 vehicles		
Catering	All excluding multiples and brewery managed public houses		

*Report of the Committee of Enquiry of Small Firms, Cmnd 4811, HMSO, 1971.

The Bolton Committee also attempted a statistical definition of a small firm. The committee recognized that while turnover was a useful size criterion for retailing, wholesaling and motor trades, employment was better for manufacturing, construction, mining and quarrying. It finally recommended eight different definitions for varying industry groups, shown in Table 1. The Bolton turnover limits have been periodically updated by an inflation index, and the latest figures are shown in the table.

Clearly there is no easy answer as to what constitutes a small firm. Not only are there conceptual problems but there are also practical problems of data availability. Any statistical analysis of small firms should be read with these problems in mind.

The distribution of small firms

A report published by the OECD in 1985 (*Employment in Small and Large Firms*) compared the extent of small firms in different OECD countries. The report showed that while small firms (defined as establishments employing fewer than 100 people) make a significant contribution to employment in Britain with 49 per cent of total employment, this is well below the average of 60 per cent for the seven

Table 2 Distribution of firms by turnover, 1985

	Turnover size (percentage of total firms)			Percentage of total business
	Up to £¼m	£¼ – £1m	£1m+	
Agriculture, forestry and fishing	91.1	8.0	0.9	9.5
Mining and quarrying and public utilities	55.5	23.3	21.1	0.1
Manufacturing	69.1	18.8	12.3	10.6
Construction	86.5	10.3	3.2	14.3
Services	83.4	11.4	5.1	65.4
All businesses	83.0	11.7	5.2	100

Source: *Midland Bank Review,* Spring 1987

OECD countries examined, and compared with 77 per cent for Japan.

The distribution of firms by turnover is presented in Table 2. This shows that over 80 per cent of firms fall into the smallest size band. The lowest proportion of small firms are in the extractive industries and public utilities, followed by manufacturing. In contrast agriculture, forestry and fishing is characterized by a high proportion of small businesses. The tradition of family ownership in agriculture largely explains the preponderance of small businesses in this sector. Small businesses are also numerous in the construction and service sectors. Small construction firms are able to operate efficiently in limited local markets, particularly in building repairs. The highest proportion of small firms amongst the service industries is to be found in catering and retailing. In contrast, small firms are less numerous in wholesaling and the motor trade, both sectors in which there are advantages to be gained from size.

Firm births and deaths

The Bolton Committee drew attention to the fact that the process of decline in the small-firms sector, which had characterized the developed countries in the post-war period, appeared to have gone further in the UK than in other countries. The committee found that the number of firms employing fewer than 200 people declined from 136 000 in 1935 to 60 000 in 1963. During the 1970s, however, a change occurred and small firms became relatively more important. this trend has continued through the 1980s, as illustrated in Table 3 which shows business registrations over the period 1980–85.

Data for Table 3 are derived from the **registration** of firms for value-added tax (VAT). New firms registering for VAT may be

Table 3 Business registrations, deregistrations and stock in the UK, 1980 – 85 (thousands)

	Stock at start of period	Registrations	Deregistrations	Net change
1980	1288	158 (12.3%)	142 (11.0%)	16 (1.2%)
1981	1304	152 (11.6%)	120 (9.2%)	32 (2.4%)
1982	1336	166 (12.4%)	146 (10.9%)	20 (1.5%)
1983	1356	180 (13.3%)	146 (10.8%)	34 (2.5%)
1984	1390	182 (13.1%)	153 (11.0%)	29 (2.1%)
1985	1419	183 (12.9%)	163 (11.5%)	20 (1.4%)
		1021	870	151 (11.7%)

The percentage figures show percentage of stock at start of period.

Source: *British Business*, 19 September 1986.

considered as firm births, with **deregistration** considered as firm deaths. It should be noted that the data are deficient in that only those businesses with a turnover above the VAT threshold need to register, so the table does not cover the smallest of the small firms. Also, deregistrations do not necessarily imply that a business has ceased to trade. Nevertheless, this is probably the best available data in the UK.

Table 3 shows that the stock of businesses increased by almost 12 per cent over the six-year period as a whole. The net change is, however, the outcome of much larger numbers of new registrations and deregistrations. On average, new registrations were over 12.5 per cent of the existing stock each year, with deregistrations averaging less than 11 per cent. There are several reasons why firms deregister. In the 1980-84 period just over 70 per cent went out of business or had a turnover below the VAT threshold limits, almost 25 per cent were taken over by other businesses, while 5 per cent simply changed their legal identity.

Business registrations by industrial sector are shown in Figure 6 for the five-year period 1980–84. This shows that all sectors with the exception of retailing experienced growth in the stock of businesses. It is thought that the reduction in the stock of retail businesses is likely to have been a reflection of the continued growth of major retailers, leading to increased concentration of activity in the sector. Those sectors experiencing the largest percentage increase in their stock of businesses includes 'other' services (30.6 per cent growth), finance, property and professional services (23.4), wholesalers (18.3), construction (17.4) and production (13.3).

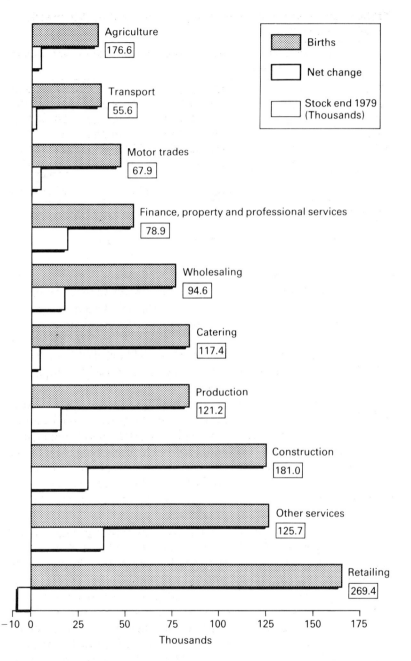

Figure 6 Business registrations 1980–84
Source: *Midland Bank Review*, Spring 1987

Reasons for growth in the number of small firms

Several explanations have been offered for the growth in the number of small firms over the 1970s and 1980s:

- Small manufacturing firms have grown in relative importance because of the decline in importance of large firms in key sectors such as motor vehicles, shipbuilding, textiles, etc.
- The relative growth of small firms reflects changes in technology, with many new technical processes being easily incorporated into smaller firms so reducing the advantages of economies of scale from which large firms formerly benefited.
- The growth of small firms reflects an increase in wealth which allows consumers to change their expenditure patterns away from standardized products, which are more likely to be produced by large firms, towards 'customized' products which are more likely to be produced by small firms.
- The rise in energy costs in the 1970s may have given an advantage to small firms which are generally less intensive users of energy than large firms.
- The growth of small firms reflects the preference of individuals for working in small firms and, in some cases, being their own boss.

Although none of these suggestions is entirely satisfactory, they at least provide an indication of the diverse factors which have influenced the relative growth in the number of small firms.

Small firm failure

Data for deregistrations over the 1974–82 period indicate the following trends:

1. In terms of the stock of businesses, annual failure rates have varied between 8 and 11 per cent, with the average over the period being just over 9 per cent a year.
2. Of those businesses that register each year, only 40 – 45 per cent will survive for a ten-year period.
3. Deregistrations are highest in the first three years of business life, with 60 per cent of deregistrations taking place in the first three years of existence.

The reasons for small firm vulnerability are many and varied:

- Small firms are often very dependent on one or two important customers or very highly specialized products, and so they are particularly at risk should one of these fail.

- Small firms are also more dependent on one or two suppliers.
- Small firms are vulnerable to any personal mishaps that may occur to the owner, such as illness or accident, which prevent him or her operating effectively.
- During a recession small firms are likely to be financially squeezed by large customers delaying payment, while suppliers and banks press hard for payment.

It is likely that personal problems and poor management constitute the most significant factors in small firm failure.

The benefits of small firms

Although the population of small firms is heterogeneous, they are thought to provide a beneficial set of functions.

As a source of competition

Small firms provide competition to larger firms in their industry, so limiting the ability of large firms to raise prices as well as encouraging them to become more efficient. It is difficult, however, to test the extent to which small firms have these desirable effects.

As a source of new jobs

One of the main reasons for government support for small firms is the belief that they are a significant generator of jobs. Much of the belief for this view came from an American study, which showed that in the USA two-thirds of *net* new jobs were created in firms employing fewer than 20 people. It should be noted, though, that these findings have been subject to much dispute.

Small firms are the seed corn from which giant companies grow

The large firms of today were once small enterprises. In most cases they grew as their industry grew, but in some cases new firms in well-established industries grew through their ability to produce lower-cost products or by supplying improved products.

It should be noted that a large number of small firms actually go out of business rather than experiencing any growth at all. Moreover, of those firms that do survive the majority will experience virtually no growth.

Small firms provide conditions for good industrial relations

A common view is that small firms can provide a working environment where owner and employees work harmoniously for their mutual benefit. Hence there are likely to be fewer industrial disputes and lower absenteeism in small firms compared with large firms.

Small firms can make a contribution to the regeneration of inner city areas

The inner cities contain heavy concentrations of the social problems of unemployment, low incomes and poor housing. It is argued that small firms can make an important contribution to the regeneration of such areas because they require relatively small sites which are available in the inner cities and use relatively labour-intensive methods of production.

Small firms are likely to be innovative

The relationship between firm size and innovation was touched on in Chapter 4, where it was noted that the role small firms play in innovation is subject to debate. Small firms do, though, produce more major inventions than large firms and often appear most willing to undertake the risks of engaging in more fundamental research activities. It is here that the link between small firms and large firms becomes important, with the small firm generating an idea and a large firm developing it commercially. The small-firm sector, therefore, has an important role to play in the innovation process.

State assistance for small firms

The government views the growth in small businesses as a major source of wealth and job creation. Part of the government's overall strategy has been the establishment of conditions for sustained growth in output and employment. A major part of this policy has involved stimulating the **supply side** of the economy and the small-firm sector in particular. The government has, therefore, promoted the ideal of entrepreneurship as a cure for high unemployment and low economic growth.

Since 1979 many new policies to promote the small-firm sector have been introduced. Broadly they can be sub-divided into financial and non-financial assistance, and their purpose is either to increase the rate at which businesses are formed or to promote the growth rate of existing businesses.

It should be noted that the following look at forms of assistance from local and national government sources does not cover the full range of measures available. Since 1979 the government has introduced over 100 policy measures relating to small firms. Given the array of assistance available it is often difficult for managers to be aware of all the possibilities. It is believed that many small firms do not obtain the help and finance they are entitled to because they are confused by the number of schemes and the often complex processes involved in making applications for assistance.

Financial assistance

Loan Guarantee Scheme
Set up in 1981, the **Loan Guarantee Scheme** (LGS) enables small firms to obtain loans from banks which they would be unable to obtain through the market, largely because the small firm is seen as a high-risk venture or the owner is unable to offer the security needed. By guaranteeing 70 per cent of the loan the government encourages banks to lend in support of viable business propositions. A premium of 2½ per cent on the guaranteed proportion of the loan is payable by the borrower. The LGS is available on amounts up to £100000, although many guarantees are issued for much smaller amounts.

One problem with the LGS is that it is expensive for the borrower, who has to pay the premium plus interest on the loan, and this limits its effectiveness.

Business Expansion Scheme
This was introduced in 1987. The key objective of the **Business Expansion Scheme** (BES) is to stimulate direct personal investment in small firms. The BES provides a tax incentive for personal investment in unquoted companies. A maximum of £40000 each year is allowable against income tax at the investor's top tax rate.

Enterprise Allowance Scheme
The **Enterprise Allowance Scheme** (EAS) is intended to help unemployed people who have a business venture in mind but who may be put off from working for themselves because they would lose entitlements to state benefits. The EAS helps to overcome this by paying an allowance of £40 per week for a year. To be eligible individuals must be over 18 and in receipt of benefits, and have been out of work for at least 8 weeks. They must also have at least £1000 to invest in the business, or be able to raise it by loan or overdraft.

Most of the businesses helped by the EAS are in the service sector and, in the initial stages at least, are 'one man firms'.

Regional and local initiatives
The Highlands and Islands Development Board, the Scottish Development Agency, the Welsh Development Agency and six local Enterprise Boards provide grants and loans for small businesses. Many local councils also provide loans and grants to assist new and small firms in their area.

Non-financial assistance

Enterprise initiatives (or consultancy)
A set of **enterprise initiatives** introduced by the Department of Trade and Industry in 1988 is designed to encourage the development of management skills through the use of outside consultancy services by small and medium-sized businesses. The firms can receive financial support towards the cost of consultancy in a number of key management functions.

Small Firms Services
There are eleven **Small Firms Service** (SFS) centres in England, two in Scotland and one in Wales. Each has a computerized database which includes all the major sources of business and government information, both national and local.

The SFS represents the government's 'one-stop shop' for advice and sources of help. The scheme provides a counselling service for small firms across a range of issues, including how to take advantage of the assistance on offer from central and local government, advice on new markets, product expansion, staff recruitment and so on.

Some case histories of satisfied clients of the SFS are reproduced at the end of this chapter.

Reducing 'red tape'
A DTI report, *Burdens on Business*, published in 1985, identified 'red tape' as a major obstacle to job creation. Government policy is now to keep the bureaucratic burdens as light as possible.

The costs of compliance with official regulations take several forms, but especially important are the costs of time of those who have to deal with officialdom and the costs of registration, licensing and making returns to the government; and such burdens fall particularly heavily on the small-firms sector.

In a White Paper, *Lifting the Burden* (1985), the government listed 70 steps it is taking to remove unnecessary burdens. These include simplifying VAT returns, employment protection and planning procedures. An Enterprise and Deregulation Unit has been established at the DTI; this is responsible for coordinating the process of regulation reform across Whitehall. All new requirements on businesses are examined to see if they are necessary – and if they are, to see how they can be implemented in a way that is cost-effective both for businesses and for the government. Gradually all existing requirements are being examined in this way.

Further details of measures to cut 'red tape' appeared in a White Paper under the title *Releasing Enterprise* in November 1988.

Other sources of assistance
Over 250 Local Enterprise Agencies provide advice and information to small firms. The Rural Development Commission Business Service, formerly known as the Council for Small Industries in Rural Areas (CoSIRA), provides technical, managerial and business advice and training to small firms in rural areas and can assist with loans. Again, many local councils provide advice and support for small firms.

Assistance from the money markets

For the majority of small businesses, the major **clearing banks** are still the most important single source of external funds. One estimate is that the four major clearing banks have about £20 billion of outstanding loans and overdrafts to businesses with a turnover of less than £1m. In addition to UK banks there are funds available from overseas banks, such as the European Investment Bank of the EEC, which provides long-term finance for small firms.

'YOU SEEM PARTICULARLY RISK-AVERSE TODAY, JULIAN.'

69

The **Unlisted Securities Market** (USM) was introduced in November 1980, to enable small and medium-sized firms more easily to obtain venture capital on the London Stock Exchange. Previously small firms were discouraged by the very high cost of a full listing on the Stock Exchange and the requirement that at least 25 per cent of shares had to be purchased by the public. The cost of joining the USM is significantly below that of a full listing, and there is a greater flexibility since companies need only place a minimum of 10 per cent of shares with the public.

Conclusions

The small-firm sector is often viewed as the embodiment of the entrepreneur. Over the past decade it has been targeted as an important source of job creation and is seen as providing a new dynamism to the economy. It is somewhat ironic, however, that a government which is apparently very committed to the operation of free markets has sought so often to intervene to assist the small business in its competitive environment.

The future prospects for small firms are not particularly clear. Their number is likely to expand, however, particularly in the service sector, and they will continue to play an important role in the economy. The recession of the early 1980s and continuing high level of unemployment gave many individuals an incentive to investigate the possibility of starting their own business. It has been argued that as more stable conditions return the country to a faster growing economy this source of incentive to start a new business will be diminished and the larger firms will reasssert themselves.

KEY WORDS

Bolton Committee	Enterprise Allowance
Registration	Scheme
Deregistration	Enterprise initiatives
Supply side	Small Firms Service
Loan Guarantee Scheme	Clearing Banks
Business Expansion	Unlisted Securities
Scheme	Market

Essay topics
1. What is a small firm?
2. Large firms are able to gain the benefits of economies of scale and

so produce more cheaply than small firms. If small firms face a cost disadvantage, why do they continue in existence?

3. What are the benefits of the small-firm sector to the UK economy?
4. Account for the growth in the number of small firms in the UK over the past decade.
5. Assess the usefulness of the various forms of official assistance available to small firms.
6. Why would a government wish to encourage the development of small businesses? How may it do so?

Reading list

Paisley, R., 'The economics of small firms', *British Economy Survey*, vol. 17, Autumn 1987, pp. 5–8.

Storey, D., 'The performance of small firms', *Economic Review*, vol. 5, Sept. 1987, pp. 28-30.

Hughes, S., Chapter 5 in *The Structure of Industry*, Collins Educational, 1988.

Data Response Question 4

The Enterprise Allowance Scheme

Read the accompanying article from the *Financial Times* of 10 August 1988 and answer the following questions.

1. How may the EAS lead to the displacement of existing employment?
2. What is meant by the 'deadweight' cost of the EAS?
3. How might the viability of a proposed business be tested?
4. Why might a viability test be a disincentive to the person eligible for the EAS?
5. Suggest ways in which the EAS may be improved in order to reduce the dropout rates and to increase the business survival rate once EAS eligibility ends.
6. Discuss the view that the introduction of the EAS had more to do with reducing the unemployment figures than with the creation of viable new businesses.
7. If the present government is sceptical of the merits of public sector intervention in the economy how can it defend the continuation of the EAS and the LGS?

Business scheme's viability found wanting

Senior officials at the Training Commission, the Government's job training agency, might be justified if they become a little dispirited by the arrival of staff from the National Audit Office at the commission's London headquarters.

Last February the NAO produced a damning report on the then Manpower Services Commission's adult training strategy.

The audit office then turned its attention to the support that the Department of Employment and the commission offers to small businesses.

Its report, published yesterday, concludes that many people becoming self-employed through the programmes would have done so anyway; a significant minority of the small businesses established merely displace existing employment; many of the concerns do not survive anyway.

The focus of the report is the Enterprise Allowance Scheme, which provides £40 a week, for a year, to anyone aged over 18 who has been unemployed for more than eight weeks and who wants to start a business. Since the scheme's national launch in August 1983, about £540m has been spent on about 325,000 entrants.

The first-year net cost to the Exchequer for each person no longer unemployed was £2,300 in 1987–88, about average for other employment schemes.

There is no test of the viability of the business proposed. The NAO acknowledges such a test could act as a disincentive, but says tests would improve the scheme's effectiveness.

The reasons are clear from the audit office's analysis of the scheme's performance.

Of the 222,900 people who entered EAS up to March 1987, 30,405 (13 per cent) dropped out before completing their year. The drop-out rate has risen as the scheme has expanded from 11 per cent in 1984–85, when there were 46,000 entrants, to about 16 per cent in 1987–88, when there were 106,000 entrants.

Of those businesses that completed the year, a quarter failed within the next six months, and most of these failures were in the first four weeks after the allowance was withdrawn. About 35 per cent of businesses failed within two years of the allowance ending.

After three years only 57 per cent of the companies were still in business.

About two-thirds of EAS entrepreneurs do not employ anyone. After three years the rate of job creation was 114 jobs (84 full-time/30 part-time) per 100 surviving firms. However, just 4 per cent of the surviving companies were responsible for 60 per cent of these additional jobs.

But these job-creation figures are a considerable over-estimate of the scheme's effect. Department of Employment surveys estimate that 44 per cent of the entrants would still have gone into self-employment without a subsidy.

Also, about half the businesses set up under EAS displace existing companies.

The impression the NAO gives of the scheme is that it helps a minority of small businesses to become viable, creating additional jobs.

A second tier of companies are one-person businesses which survive for some time, but about 38 per cent entail one burst of self-employment, with no checks on how the weekly £40 is being spent.

		ENTERPRISE ALLOWANCE SCHEMES			
Year	Expendi- ture (£m)	Target no. entrants	Entrants	Drop-outs	Drop-out rate (%)
1984–85	77	50,000	46,000	5,050	11.0
1985–86	104	62,500	60,000	7,500	13.0
1986–87	143	85,900	86,800	13,450	16.5
1987–88	196	102,500	105,300	17,000	18.0
Totals	545		329,200	47,405	

Along with viability tests, as well as better business training, the audit office recommends a series of other measures to target support on those most likely to succeed.

These themes are echoed by the office's analysis of the Department's Loan Guarantee Scheme under which the Government guarantees 70 per cent of a loan made by a bank to someone starting a business. The aim is to help small companies which would not otherwise get a start-up loan, because they lack a track record.

The Government had intended the scheme to be self-financing. But by last year, after six years, 17,648 loans worth £579m had been guaranteed, at a net cost to the Government of £109m.

Loans worth £146m had been written off as bad debts, and income raised through charging borrowers a premium over the interest charged by the bank, had only come to £37m.

An audit office analysis of the last official follow-up survey of the businesses set up under the scheme found that more than half would have got bank loans without the LGS.

The report says this means about three additional jobs are created per loan, and that less than 10 per cent of the companies created almost half these jobs.

Charles Leadbeater

Data Response Question 5

A visit to the bank manager

Read the accompanying article from the *Financial Times* of 11 February 1989, which was written by a divisional manager of Lloyds Bank Small Business Services. Answer the following questions.

1. Although 'feared and unloved', bank managers are keen to lend money. Why?
2. What would make a 'Crocodile Fight Training Centre' a viable business?
3. Explain how 'debt servicing ability' is a problem common to an entrepreneur in a start-up firm, a family with heavy 'plastic money' borrowings and an A-level student who has overspent his or her personal allowance.

Minding your own business

Bank managers often feel like the beast – as in Beauty and the Beast. We believe we are feared and unloved undeservedly despite our natural warmth and affection.

As for helping small businesses or business start-ups, it is true that we do sometimes have to seek further information and even turn down requests for loans on the basis that bank finance is not appropriate for the scheme concerned, or that the business cannot generate sufficient income to repay, or even that the scheme itself is completely dotty.

I would point out, though, that just because you think crocodile wrestling is the greatest relaxation imaginable, it does not follow automatically that spending £100,000 on a Crocodile Fight Training Centre is a viable business initiative.

One of my favourite encounters was with a charming and persistent customer who had no job or income but who wanted funds to travel to South America in order to start a silver mine. He was supremely confident of success; I felt that Lloyds Bank shareholders might see things differently. When I said: "No, no, no, definitely not, under any circumstances," his confident response was: "Well, can I speak to someone who can make a decision?" He reminded me of the football manager looking for "a result."

The truth is that bank managers *like* to help, because a satisfied customer is an excellent source of new business. Small businesses make satisfying customers as problems are shared with them. And, of course, we do need to make a profit.

While there can be no cast-iron guaranteed way to obtain funds from a bank, some carefully considered plans, with assumptions which have been tested thoroughly go a long way to help.

Looking at things from the bank manager's point of view, he has a business to develop, too. With increasing competition, existing customers have to be retained and new ones wooed.

Don't try to persuade the bank manager to say "yes" to a shaky proposition. That doesn't do anyone any good. The business plan (an almost mandatory document these days before the serious talking starts) must lend substance to the proposal. It must support the people involved, give credibility to the declared aims, and set out answers clearly to questions that the manager could only discover otherwise after a long interview.

Presentation is important when going to the bank for money, although perhaps not in the way you might think. Glossy productions, bound expensively, with artists' impressions of the proposed factory, do little to win the bank manager's heart. I once told a group of accountants that I would rather see a few figures scribbled on an envelope by the proprietor of the business than a 100-page "glossy." They showed some incredulity, but I think I made the point that the medium must not be allowed to take over the message.

It is also a good idea to be familiar with the contents of the business plan and other information you are offering to support your quest for cash. It is not at all helpful to the bank manager if you answer his questions with: "Oh, you'll have to ask my accountant that, he prepared the plan."

Cynics say that cash flow forecasts always have three features: they forecast peak borrowing in the first month, restoration to credit within nine months and a substantial positive balance by the end of the year.

It is surprising how many do look like that, presumably on the ill – conceived basis of "let's spend the goodies as soon as possible and tempt

the bank manager by showing him what a good account it will be within 12 months." That will not work, I can tell you.

Your manager will study carefully certain areas in your plan. These are:

• **The early months.** The purposes of the initial drawings of the loan are vital. New BMWs for the proprietor and his family will not impress the bank half as much as they will the neighbours. A display of prudence at a time when funds are in short supply in those early days is far more likely to win the manager's support.

• **Always come clean.** If you think you can raise additional finance without the bank's knowledge, forget it. Borrowing to cover the deposit on equipment to be bought on hire-purchase (or advance rental on leasing transactions) will raise questions about the debt. The equity level, or debt servicing ability, must be realistic.

• **The top line.** The "bottom line" is an expression that has become a cliche for modern life outside the financial world. What is important in forecasts, however, is the top line –

the sales projection. If this turns out to be adrift hopelessly, the cash projection will collapse in ruins, too.

The bank manager will need to be entirely comfortable with the figures, the assumptions behind them, and the projected time – lag between sales and collection of the debts. If there is a simple, most important part of the whole business plan, then that is it.

A good sales projection follows from analysis of the market and the competition, the range of potential customers, etc. It is vital because it affects the profit and loss account, the repayment of bank borrowing, and, ultimately, the growth of the business.

Finally, a tip. Don't regard your business plan simply as a means of borrowing money from the bank. Use it as a continuing source of reference for monitoring your business activity. If you exercise the discipline of self-monitoring, and take the trouble to tell your bank manager when real life is diverging from the plan, it will demonstrate that the business is being run properly – and do wonders for your credibility.

CASE HISTORIES: Clients of the Small Firms Service

The three short excerpts reproduced here are taken from the annual report of the Small Firms Service for 1987–88.

* * *

Concorde Couriers, Teddington, London

A handful of booklets on how to set up in business collected from the Small Firms Centre gave Simon Bliss the basis for starting his successful motorbike messenger service, which in 1987 had a turnover of £1.3 million and a staff of 100.

Ten years ago, aged 21, Simon had been a Civil Service clerk and an advertising salesman. With the help of the SFS booklets, he started Concord Couriers with £500 capital, a car, use of a friend's motorbike and his parent's spare bedroom. Turnover in the first year grossed £25000. Then the business began to grow faster than Simon could handle.

'I was doing all the jobs,' he explains, 'managing the office, marketing delivering, the lot. I went back to the Small Firms Service and they put me in touch with a Counsellor who showed me the need to distance myself from the day-to-day operation and establish a management structure.'

With the new organization, Concord Couriers continued to grow and now has four offices in the north west, south and centre of London, providing a capital-wide service.

Rainbow Enterprises, Sabden, near Blackburn

Having a great idea is one thing. Recognizing its full potential is quite another.

Bill Dewhurst started in business on the Enterprise Allowance Scheme selling soft toys. These were a range of characters based on local history and folklore called the Sabden Treacle Miners. Each toy sold with a story featuring that character and there was soon a demand for children to visit the non-existent treacle mines.

SFS Counsellor Margaret Carmichael-Grimshaw helped Bill to identify the enormous potential, clarify ways of exploiting it, locate a possible site for a theme park and bring together local planners, the Tourist Board and potential investors to develop the idea. Other spin-offs are a TV series, teeshirts and food products.

Bill, now managing director of Rainbow Enterprises, has a high regard for Margaret's advice concerning the next stage of the company's development.

Stephen Hunter Stained Glass, South Elmsall, West Yorkshire

Counselling by the Small Firms Service can be a continuing process, from start-up to growth and success.

Stephen Hunter first saw an SFS Counsellor one week after he had started his business under the Enterprise Allowance Scheme in September 1985. The Counsellor's verdict was that Stephen was already selling himself into bankruptcy by charging prices that were far too low. A simple costing system was suggested and adopted and a sensible business plan drawn up with special attention to marketing.

It could be any business, but Stephen was an artist in stained glass and his product was custom-built stained-glass windows. The business became strong enough for Jill, his wife, to give up her job, take over the office work and do simple designs for mirrors and frames.

A second SFS counselling session six months later updated the business plan to cover stronger marketing, including higher prices, a move to an industrial unit from his home, employment of a YTS and a craft trainee, and investment in productive equipment. By early 1987, the business employed six people and turnover was £50000 a year.

Later that year, the Small Firms Service introduced Stephen to the Support for Marketing Initiative of the Department of Trade and Industry. This helped to pay for a management consultant with experience in consumer marketing in the areas of craft, design and colour. The result was a marketing strategy aiming for a turnover of £200000 plus.

Chapter Eight
Entrepreneurship and the large corporation

Managers can only ensure their own security if the firm is secure, and this is associated with profitability and growth.

It is a commonly held view that entrepreneurship is invariably most visible in the small firm. It is the small firm that is recognized as best exhibiting risk-taking, innovation and profit maximization. In contrast, the large firm is characterized as minimizing its exposure to risk through mergers and diversification, reacting to, rather than creating, innovation, and maximizing such objectives as sales revenue and management salaries rather than profit. Moreover, it is the small firm and not the large enterprise which is viewed as providing the competitive impetus to economic development.

Guardians of the status quo

The view that the natural habitat of entrepreneurs is small businesses and that they are rarely found in large corporations is supported by the argument that, when a company grows beyond some critical size, its increased complexity forces it to replace its venturesome founders with professional managers who are not usually noted for their innovative risk-taking behaviour. Rather, professional managers are the guardians and conservators of the status quo. While entrepreneurs are quick to see possibilities for achievement, managers in large staid organizations are blinded by the ingrown **bureaucratic culture** in which they are embedded.

Others argue, however, that the widespread belief that entrepreneurship is more aggressively pursued in the small business sector of the economy than in that of the large corporation is held without any empirical evidence to support it. Accepting that there are aggressive entrepreneurs among the small business units, it is maintained that there are other firms which have taken few risks since their act of foundation. Indeed, there are hundreds of small enterprises which survive with little alteration over time in product range or manufacturing and distribution methods. Although technically entrepreneurs, they display little sign of entrepreneurial thrust. They have no desire to push beyond their present horizons and within this constraint they perform their necessary functions in a modest fashion.

Vigorous entrepreneurial pursuits are thus not the prerogative of the small business, nor is ultra-conservatism to be found only in large corporations. Further, there is no proof that high-risk, high-return projects will be rejected by the management of large concerns in favour of low-risk, low-return investments. The basic nature of certain industries even precludes a choice between the two. In the exploration for crude oil, for example, the costs are high and the odds against success of single ventures are substantial; when search culminates in the discovery of an oilfield, however, the rewards can be massive.

Over recent years there has been a growing view that it is possible – and indeed necessary – for entrepreneurship to flourish within large business organizations. This chapter discusses the main elements of this view.

Entrepreneurial management

It is maintained that senior management of modern business enterprises must perform creatively, are compelled to take risks and are induced to innovate – by their competitors, their customers and their own search for successful personal achievement. As such, even in the absence of the element of ownership, they perform as entrepreneurs. Although for many observers the so-called divorce of ownership and management has apparently signalled the end of entrepreneurship in large-scale business, here it is argued that only if entrepreneurship is interpreted narrowly as sole ownership of the enterprise is it appropriate to discuss the end of entrepreneurship.

'Entrepreneurial management' is creative, innovative and risk-taking management, where taking of risks and initiating enterprise is a basic part of management's search for certainty and security. The motivation of managers to perform successfully is determined by the promise of security in their jobs. Managers can only ensure their own security if the firm is secure, and this is associated with profitability and the growth of the firm. The management team, in order to secure their income, must ensure the survival and growth of the firm, and this they do by formulating policies of creativity, innovation and risk-taking.

Hence, although the large-scale business is inescapably bureaucratic, the continuing activities of the business must remain entrepreneurial if the business is to survive and grow. Unlike the act of business formation, however, where the creativity and innovation is usually the responsibility of a single individual, such creativity and innovation must be the responsibilities of all the key individuals or policy-makers of the now complicated business organization. Indeed, the development of **corporate strategy** depends on the combination of entrepreneurship and management, and this combination requires from the firm a structure of entrepreneurial management.

Strategic management

Determining the strategy of a business is only one of the functions of management. It is, though, the most significant area of top management decision-making. Strategic management is concerned with arriving at decisions on what the organization ought to be doing and where it should be going. Strategic decisions are concerned with the relationship between the firm and the external environment in which it operates, and involve determining what kind of business the firm should seek to be in. Successful entrepreneurial management is observed primarily as the formulation of effective corporate strategy. In other words, corporate policy-making is essentially an entrepreneurial activity.

The practice of entrepreneurship

Entrepreneurship is based on the same priorities, whether the entrepreneur is in an existing large institution or an individual starting his or her own venture single-handed. The roles are essentially the same: the things that will and will not work are basically the same, as are the kinds of innovation and where to look for them.

Yet the existing large business faces problems, limitations and constraints that are different from those of the solo entrepreneur, and it needs to learn different things. In particular, established corporations need a specific guide to the practice of entrepreneurship: businesses must *learn* to manage themselves for entrepreneurship because entrepreneurship is not natural or spontaneous. However, there are a substantial number of existing businesses, among them a significant number of large ones, that succeed as innovators and entrepreneurs, which clearly indicates that entrepreneurship and innovation may be achieved by any business. It must be consciously striven for.

Management buy-outs

One aspect of entrepreneurship in large companies which has become common place during the 1980s is that of the management buy-out. This occurs where the management team of a company 'buys-out' the

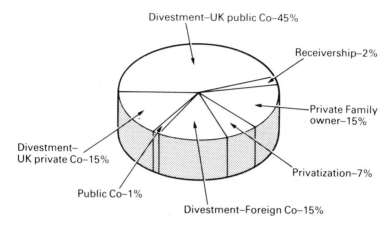

WHO IS SELLING?

Divestment–UK public Co–45%

Receivership–2%

Private Family owner–15%

Divestment–UK private Co–15%

Public Co–1%

Privatization–7%

Divestment–Foreign Co–15%

Sources of buy-outs – % of the total number 1986

Source: *Financial Weekly*, 12th November 1988

Figure 7   An analysis of management buy-outs during 1986, according to *Financial Weekly*, 12 November 1988

existing owner or owners and takes over the control of the business themselves. Figure 7 shows the sources of management buy-outs for 1986, that is the type of companies selling out to their managements. The largest source of management buy-out are divestments of subsidiaries, either from UK or foreign firms. Many of the UK's top industrial and commercial groups have divested themselves of several companies through management buy-outs. These include firms such as Hanson Trust, GKN, ASDA, STC, RTZ, P & O, Unilever and Thorn EMI. Other sources of buy-out occur when a firm goes into receivership and when a family or private firm is bought out by management. An interesting, although relatively small component of buy-outs results from Government decisions to privatize; this occurred for example, in the buy-out of the National Freight Corporation in 1982.

Table 4 shows that the number of management buy-outs has increased in number and value through the 1980s.

Table 4

ON THEIR OWN
Total number and value of
buy-outs 1967–1988

Year	no.	Value (£m)	Average Value (£m)
1967–76	43	–	–
1977	13	–	–
1978	23	–	–
1979	52	26	0.50
1980	107	50	0.47
1981	124	114	0.92
1982	170	265	1.56
1983	205	315	1.54
1984	210	415	1.98
1985	229	1,150	5.02
1986	261	1,210	4.64
1987	300	2,820	9.4
1988 (to 15 Sept.)	210	2,330	11.1
Total	1,747	8,695	

Buy-out value on the rise

Source: *Financial Weekly* and *Investor Chronicle*

Intrapreneurship

A relatively new view of entrepreneurship within the large corporation is the notion of the intrapreneur, which is shorthand for 'intracorporate entrepreneur'. Intrapreneuring is seen as a revolutionary system for speeding up innovation within large firms by making better use of their entrepreneurial talent. A company can then hold on to its best innovators by providing them with the opportunity to make their ideas happen without having to leave the company and perhaps set up as competitors. From the standpoint of the company the benefits of having intrapreneurs are obvious: intrapreneurs introduce and produce new products and processes which in turn enable the company as a whole to grow and improve profits.

For the would-be innovator the resources available within a large corporation can be attractive. Corporations can provide manufacturing facilities, networks of supportive suppliers, access to technology, personnel resources and manufacturing expertise. Such advantages are, though, often offset by bureaucratic systems that inhibit intrapreneurship. Many new entrepreneurs leave corporations because they feel frustrated in their attempt to innovate, not because they find their pay and benefits insufficient. Hence, it is argued, intrapreneurs need the freedom to act within organizations as much as they need material compensation.

Corporate entrepreneurs, despite prior successes, have no capital of their own to start other ventures. Officially, they must begin from scratch by pursuading management that their new ideas are promising. Intrapreneurs' inability to use the earnings from one success to fund the next is among the greatest barriers to intrapreneuring. It has been suggested that to overcome this a new system of rewards be devised, including '**intra-capital**', which is a fund set aside by the corporation for use by a specific intrapreneur to start new businesses on behalf of the corporation.

Although some major companies have adopted this type of intrapreneurial model, in broad terms it is somewhat idealistic – the conflict between freedom and control is inherent and permanent in all organizations. It is probably right to argue, however, that the corporate balance needs to be tipped towards freedom, with the greater encouragement of innovation and entrepreneurial flair of the corporate employees.

Conclusions

Once an entrepreneur has established a company and taken it through a period of growth – with resultant increase in size and complexity – the conventional view is that at this point the firm needs to undergo a transformation to more formal management systems, with the original entrepreneur playing a peripheral role. The increased bureaucracy of mature firms under professional management has, for some observers, signalled the end of entrepreneurship in established firms.

There is a growing school of thought which argues, however, that professional management, as traditionally conceived, will seek to be entrepreneurial anyway, as their personal security lies in the security of the firm. This is associated with increased profits and growth which accrue from acquiring and responding to opportunities in the environment.

Intrapreneurship, meanwhile, concentrates on the individual within the firm, and offers a recipe for successful innovation within the established firm by providing the necessary freedoms and incentives for those with entrepreneurial traits.

```
                        KEY WORDS

    Bureaucratic culture            Intrapreneurship
    Entrepreneurial management      Intra-capital
    Corporate strategy
```

Reading list

Drucker, P.F., *'Innovational Entrepreneurship: Practice and Principles'*, Heinemann, 1985

Essay topics

1. Is it in the interest of a top manager in a large company to act in an entrepreneurial manner?
2. 'Small firms embody entrepreneurship while large firms embody bureaucratic management. Small firms are thus more likely to be innovative.' Discuss this statement.
3. Compare and contrast an entrepreneur with an intrapreneur.
4. 'The divorce of ownership from management in large companies spells the end of the entrepreneur.' Discuss.

PROFILE: Art Fry of the 3M Company

Art Fry of the US company 3M is the inventor and intrapreneur of Post-it Notes, which are little yellow notepads with a peelable sticky surface along the top of the back side. Fry made use not only of 3M's corporate funds but also of its technology and existing pilot plants, manufacturing facilities and marketing channels. This access to corporate money and expertise was important to his success, but equally important was strong, loyal sponsorship within 3M: for example, Fry's immediate supervisor was a strong backer throughout the development in which Fry worked.

Fry began working on Post-it Notes in 1974 while in church. He sang in the choir and would mark the selected hymns in his hymn book with slips of paper. These bookmarks worked quite well but some of the markers would fall out. Fry decided that he needed a marker that would adhere to the page but not damage it when it was removed. Taking advantage of 3M's policy that allows a technical personnel 15 per cent of their work time to develop ideas of their own, Fry began to work on a prototype peelable bookmark.

A weak adhesive had already been developed by 3M which had no readily identifiable use. Samples of the new adhesive had been distributed within the company in the hope that someone would discover a use for it. As there were bottles of the adhesive available Fry made himself some peelable markers for his hymn book.

A particular difficulty with a new idea is that it is often difficult to describe to others. With Post-it Notes, until the management in 3M could gain some understanding of its application – how it could stick and be removable as well as how it could assist individuals at work or in the home – they could not develop any feeling for the opportunity that was available.

Another significant barrier that Fry had to overcome was finding a process to coat this new adhesive on paper so that it performed properly. Controlling the stickiness proved extremely difficult and Fry found himself with little support within 3M. Those responsible for manufacturing thought the product would be impossible to produce because the process could not be controlled. Fry remained optimistic.

When the necessary equipment in other divisions was not required Fry obtained use of it. Fry worked with great dedication, often at night. When he received official permission to use a pilot plant he worked five consecutive eight-hour shifts (i.e. 40 hours) without stopping. He relentlessly pursued his goal of a workable process for making Post-it Notes. In the end, however, Fry was left with a good product idea but one which was impossible to manufacture using existing 3M technology.

Fry would not accept defeat. He invented a machine that would manufacture the product. When the manufacturing engineers at 3M told Fry that the machine he had designed would take six months to build and cost a considerable amount of money, he reacted by building a prototype in his basement and had it installed and working inside 3M within a week.

Just as the manufacturing process was solved another problem arose. Surveys by the marketing department discovered that people said they did not see the need for paper with a weak adhesive on it. This response poses a difficulty for any intrapreneur with a new product. If something is so new and different that people are unable to imagine how to use it, then a survey will usually show that they do not need it. This does not necessarily mean that the product is a poor one – only that people have to use it before they realize how useful it is. Despite the fact that marketing surveys continued to show that people had no interest, Fry's own experience of people's use and requests for more pads within the 3M company convinced him that there was a sizeable market.

Fry's determination in establishing an economical production process and his ability to satisfy 3M that there was a market for the product eventually led to its launch. Through direct sales demonstrations and promotional free samples, sales began to grow. Eventually Post-it Notes became an international success for 3M.

PROFILE: Lord Weinstock of the General Electric Company

Lord Weinstock, the son of Polish immigrants, is considered by some to be the greatest industrialist of the epoch. Both his parents died before he reached the age of nine and he was brought up by the eldest of his five brothers. He studied for a degree in statistics at the LSE. In 1947 he met his wife who was the daughter of a maker of television and radio sets.

Five years after marriage Weinstock went into business with his father-in-law making television sets at Radio and Allied Industries. It was there that he developed his remarkable skill at controlling a business and first demonstrated his fanatical devotion to curbing waste. One considerable saving he made on TV cabinets was through the discovery of a man making church pews in Scotland whose knowledge of treating veneer allowed Radio and Allied to make a highly competitive reduction in costs.

Weinstock's significant ambition in the late 1960s and early 1970s was to create a major electronics and electrical group. This desire sparked the acquisition of Associated Electrical Industries in 1967 and the merger with the English Electric Company one year later. A general mopping up of smaller companies over the following years gave GEC pride of place amongst electronic companies. It is widely accepted that Weinstock's successful implementation of these mergers and the resulting rationalization of large parts of the electrical engineering industry in Britain was a monumental achievement.

GEC's success in the 1970s lay in winning a series of lucrative contracts from successive governments in defence and public sector areas. Many of these were awarded on a 'cost plus' basis, which means that a customer has to meet all the contractor's costs, plus a fixed profit percentage on top. Thus Weinstock hit on a successful formula for making money. By selling principally to government bodies who were prepared to tolerate the cost-plus pricing rule, keeping GEC's plant running at full capacity, not replacing old technology and keeping costs high, Weinstock increased GEC's turnover four times from 1971 to 1981.

Weinstock's personality and presence have always heavily influenced the development of the company, not only in terms of length of service – which in itself exceeds that of all other chairmen or managing directors at companies of the size of GEC – but in terms of the particular character which he has stamped on the group. Weinstock is extremely prudent, with a passion for eliminating waste. The result of this prudence has been the build-up of huge cash resources totalling £1.23 billion in 1989. This has led to criticism against Weinstock, who it is alleged has failed to reinvest GEC's cash in new technologies.

GEC unsuccessfully bid for Plessey in 1986, the proposed merger being overruled by the Monopolies and Mergers Commission. In late 1988 GEC, together with Siemens of West Germany, jointly bid £1.76 billion for Plessey, and this was again referred to the MMC. This bid led to the formation of a consortium of companies including Plessey, under the umbrella company of Metsun, who bid £7 billion for GEC with the intention of breaking it up.

In the wake of this bid Weinstock announced a number of joint-venture agreements:

- with General Electric of the USA in the domestic appliance market
- with Siemens of West Germany in defence and telecommunications
- with Alsthom of France in power engineering.

It has been argued that General Electric, in siding with GEC and not with the Metsun consorium, considerably reduced the likelihood that GEC would be taken over.

Chapter Nine
Conclusions

Relatively recent shifts in economic policy have made an understanding of the nature of the entrepreneur increasingly important. The supply side policies adopted by the Thatcher administration during the 1980s are clearly designed to foster an entrepreneurial response. Reductions in the rates of direct taxation, for example, have been partly to enhance incentives so as to create an atmosphere in which enterprise can flourish, while the process of privatization – the transfer of state industries to the private sector – it is claimed, have sharply improved the performance of the former state industries through management having to respond to the discipline of the competitive market place. In general the government has placed considerable emphasis on increasing competition in all sectors of the economy and in inculcating entrepreneurial attitudes. These themes are taken up in comparison volumes in this series: in particular see *Privatization and the Public Sector* by Bryan Hurl, *Supply Side Economics* by Rosalind Levačić and *Mrs Thatcher's Economics* by David Smith.

A similar, although significantly much more limited, move towards encouraging initiative and enterprise has also occurred in the Soviet Union under Mr Gorbachev's system of economic reforms as part of the *perestroika* or reconstruction of the Soviet system. In essence the aim of the economic reforms is to nudge the Soviet Union towards a system of market socialism. The main change so far has been to abolish some of the Russian government's millions of production directives. Under Soviet planning all factories received their orders from Moscow and prices were kept unchanged for decades. From the beginning of 1989 a new set of laws came into force reducing the role of central planners and switching enterprises to self-management. The enterprises are now able to deal with each other and set their own prices, and if they are not profitable they will have to lay off staff, reduce wages or even close. Gorbachev's economic reform programme faces obstacles, however. Stubborn bureaucrats have resisted change at all levels, while the business managers have been at a loss to know how to take initiatives after decades of blindly following directives.

Given the new importance of these various economic policies in trying to stimulate enterprise and initiative, it is rather disappointing that economists have reached no real concensus on the role of the entrepreneur in the economy. The standard economic theory of the firm operating under conditions of perfect competition provides no place at all for the entrepreneur. Despite this a commonly held view is that the entrepreneur is the economic agent who shoulders the burden of risks in supplying goods and obtains the reward of profit for doing so. This appears to be the view which underlies the supply side approach. As Rosalind Levačić has written, 'entrepreneurs are motivated by the expectation of profit to discover and supply products that consumers want and to use efficient production methods.'

As Chapter 4 shows this is an enduring view of the entrepreneur, but there are other approaches. Schumpeter stressed the relationship between entrepreneurship and innovation, where the carrying out of new combinations will disturb markets and move them away from equilibrium, but in doing so will generate economic growth. In contrast others, in particular the Austrian school of economists, emphasize the role of the entrepreneur in bringing markets towards equilibrium by being perceptive and alert to profit opportunities. Much of the recent emphasis on the supply side approach to economic policy has been on the encouragement of new and small businesses. It should also be noted, however, that the entrepreneurial function is increasingly seen to be part of the large business organization and is not confined to new firms or the running of small and medium-sized enterprises.

Index